# Language and Power
## in the Early Middle Ages

Patrick J. Geary

# Language & Power in the Early Middle Ages

THE MENAHEM STERN JERUSALEM LECTURES

*Brandeis
University
Press*

*Historical
Society
of Israel*

BRANDEIS UNIVERSITY PRESS
WALTHAM, MASSACHUSETTS

Brandeis University Press
Historical Society of Israel
An imprint of
University Press of New England
www.upne.com
© 2013 Historical Society of Israel
All rights reserved
Manufactured in the
United States of America
Designed by Sara Rutan
Typeset in Dante Pro by Integrated Publishing Solutions

University Press of New England is a
member of the Green Press Initiative.
The paper used in this book meets their
minimum requirement for recycled paper.

For permission to reproduce any of the
material in this book, contact Permissions,
University Press of New England, One
Court Street, Suite 250, Lebanon NH 03766;
or visit www.upne.com

Library of Congress Cataloging-in-Publication Data
Geary, Patrick J., 1948–
Language and power in the early Middle Ages / Patrick J. Geary.
    p. cm. — (The Menahem Stern Jerusalem Lectures)
Includes bibliographical references and index.
ISBN 978-1-61168-390-5 (cloth: alk. paper) — ISBN 978-1-61168-391-2
(pbk.: alk. paper) — ISBN 978-1-61168-392-9 (ebook)
    1. Language and history. 2. Middle Ages. 3. Language and culture.
4. Language and languages—Philosophy—Early works to 1800. I. Title.

P41.G34 2013
401—dc23

2012032043

5  4  3  2  1

# Contents

# Foreword

YITZHAK HEN

It is a great pleasure and a considerable honor to welcome Professor Patrick J. Geary to Jerusalem on behalf of the Historical Society of Israel.

To introduce Professor Geary in a short note is simply impossible. Just to list the various honors conferred upon him or to recite his list of publications will leave no space for him to deliver his own lectures. Hence, all I can do in the short space allocated to me is to give you my own personal, and rather impressionistic, appreciation of Professor Geary and his work.

Let me begin with the concluding episode of one of Hollywood's masterpieces—*The Godfather, Part II* (1974)—in which Michael Corleone was investigated by a Senate committee, but found not guilty because witnesses could not be brought forth to testify against him. One member of this committee, a sinister and corrupt senator from Nevada, apparently an ally of Michael Corleone, gave a passionate speech in support of Italian Americans, before leaving the room in a dramatic move. This senator was called Patrick Geary, and this is the image I had in mind when, more than twenty years ago, I picked up a book titled *Furta Sacra* and read it for the first time. As a young student, who had just started his stroll on the dark paths of the early Middle Ages, I was fascinated by this lucid and provocative book, and so I decided to read everything written by Patrick Geary that I could lay my hands upon. Funnily enough, the more I read, the more my image of Patrick Geary as Don Corleone's court historian was crystallized, for he wrote about the theft of relics; the humiliation of saints; honor, vendettas, and blood feuds among the Merovingians; and living with the dead in the Middle Ages. Everything fell neatly into place. But then, in 1996, I met Patrick Geary in person, and my delightful image was shattered. What I found in front of me was a cheerful person, a devoted teacher, and a generous and most amicable colleague and friend.

Professor Geary is well known to medievalists for his groundbreaking work on the early and central Middle Ages. For more than four decades, Professor Geary has written with sustained intelligence, opening up new subjects and contributing lucid and comprehensive analyses to the discussion of many religious, social, and cultural issues, such as the cults of relics, memory and oblivion, and the medieval concepts of the past. His numerous articles and books combine detailed scrutiny of primary sources with larger insights into the world in which various phenomena occurred. More recently, Professor Geary has turned, *inter alia*, to the study of medieval foundation myths and their use (or, rather, abuse) in modern Europe.

Throughout his published work, Professor Geary stands at the forefront of medieval historiography. The subjects on which he has written were the most intensely debated topics at the time, and his contributions to these debates were always innovative, thought provoking, and challenging, rather than traditional. In the late 1970s, when scholars were ecstatic about saints and their cults, Patrick Geary wrote *Furta Sacra: Thefts of Relics in the Central Middle Ages* (1978, rev. ed. 1990), telling us about the thefts of relics—or, more precisely, about the invention of theft stories to justify the authenticity of some newly discovered relics. In the mid 1980s, Patrick Geary wrote his magisterial book *Aristocracy in Provence: The Rhône Basin at the Dawn of the Carolingian Age* (1985), combining the old tradition of writing history from a legal, institutional, and social viewpoint with the perspectives of social sciences that gradually took over the writing of social history at the time. In the late 1980s, when Merovingian history became extremely popular in France and the United Kingdom, Geary wrote his *Before France and Germany: The Creation and Transformation of the Merovingian World* (1988), striving to do away with some of the most influential myths that surrounded the Merovingians and their role in history. In the early 1990s, when memory became the flashiest topic among medievalists, following the publication of Michael T. Clanchy's *From Memory to Written Record* (1979, 2nd ed. 1993) and Mary Carruthers's *The Book of Memory* (1990), Patrick Geary wrote *Phantoms of Remembrance: Memory and Oblivion at the End of the First Millennium* (1994). Finally, in the late 1990s and the early years of the current millennium, when ethnicity became seminal in any discussion of the post-Roman world, Patrick Geary wrote *The Myths of Nations: The Medieval Origins of Europe* (2002), focusing not so much on barbarian ethnicity and early medieval foundation myths, but rather on their use in a modern, nationalistic context. There is always something refreshing, original, and unconventional in Professor Geary's work, and this witty twist is, to my mind, what makes him one of the most interesting scholars of our generation.

Inviting Professor Geary to deliver the Fifteenth Annual Lectures in memory of Menahem Stern is just a small token of appreciation of his work and his long-lasting friendship with many Israeli scholars. By accepting this invitation, Professor Geary confirmed yet again the high respect with which the Stern Lectures are being held among historians throughout the world.

# Introduction

Language, for at least the past two centuries, has come to be seen as a fundamental marker of identity. Linguistic communities are taken as synonymous with ethnic and national communities, particularly in competing identity politics in which different interest groups are mobilized by appeals to presumably fundamental and primordial differences. Language is widely understood to transmit the fundamental cultural, social, and political values of a people, and differences in language are understood as the most obvious markers of internal solidarity and external difference.[1] In the United States, advocates of "English only" promote the designation of English as the official language of the United States and oppose the use of other languages in education and in government offices and services. At the same time politicians seeking to create voting blocs of immigrants and their descendants from such diverse societies as Cuba, Puerto Rico, the Dominican Republic, Mexico, the American Southwest, and South America call into being a "Hispanic" community, as if the bond of the mother tongue of all of these diverse populations were more significant than their very different ethnic, colonial, national, cultural, and educational backgrounds. In Canada, Francophone and Anglophone differences have regularly led to tensions that at times have threatened to break the country apart, while in Europe the continuing linguistic crisis in Belgium between Walloons and Flemish, particularly focused on the multilinguistic city of Brussels and its suburbs, may well bring about an end to this nation at the heart of Europe. Linguistic separatism in the Iberian Peninsula, and particularly the tensions between Barcelona and Madrid, continue to be a source of tension, while in the Baltic, language is the primary battleground over the fate of Russian minorities in these newly independent states. The situation is particularly critical in Estonia, where descendants of Russians who emigrated after 1940 to what was then the Estonian Soviet Socialist Republic are denied citizenship unless they can pass an Estonian language examination.

The importance of language for national identity is of course central in the history of Zionism and need hardly be rehearsed for readers. From the tentative and highly artificial attempts to revive Hebrew as a literary language in nineteenth-century Europe to the revival of spoken Hebrew in Palestine largely through the efforts of Eliezer Ben Yehuda, the successful revival—one might even say the invention—of modern Hebrew as a living language spoken by millions of people is an extraordinary achievement. But it must not be forgotten that the linguistic nationalist movement of Ben Yehuda was but a particular manifestation of a much broader contemporary European nationalist ideology that defined national language as an indispensable attribute of nationhood. By 1881, when Ben Yehuda arrived in Jerusalem, the coincidence of nation and language had become an accepted fact of political and cultural life, and he shared with other European intellectuals the assumption that a single nation required a single language.

But of course language need not be spoken by a population to play a powerful role in national politics. Communities can make language a symbolic marker of difference, even if it is not the actual language of the community. The Basque language, for example, a powerful symbol in the continuing struggle of the Basque population for greater autonomy, is actually spoken by perhaps no more than 30 percent of the population of Spanish Basque country.[2] The constitution of the Republic of Ireland declares Irish to be the national language although, in spite of a century of efforts to revive and standardize Irish, under 10 percent of Ireland's population uses the language actively.

And of course language is, in our own day, often irrelevant in both internal and external disputes that pit one community against another: sectarianism, not language, bitterly divides Catholic and Protestant communities in Northern Ireland and Shi'ia and Sunni communities in Iraq; and in North America and, increasingly, in Europe, race and religion rather than language divide populations.

Language, then, is only one of the cultural artifacts that under specific circumstances can be mobilized (one is tempted to say "weaponized") for political action. We are acutely aware of this in the present, and yet we often forget it when examining Europe's past. We have come to think of linguistic communities as somehow natural, even primordial, and we take it for granted that the history of the linguistic diversity of Europe from antiquity to the high Middle Ages is indicative of the history of Europe's peoples.

Every story has its back story, and the history of European nations and national languages in the nineteenth century is no exception. In spite of attempts by modern sociologists to claim that the nation and national identities are the invention of the late eighteenth and early nineteenth centuries, national discourses have a very deep history, reaching into the Middle Ages. But of course the essence of history is change over time, not immutability. These premodern discourses, even while

evoking nations and communities, did so with radically different understandings of the nature of such communities and of
the place of language in these constructions. Language, in the
Middle Ages, was assumed to be but one element in the identity
of a people. To quote the tenth-century abbot and chronicler
Regino of Prüm (died ca. 915), peoples differ from one another
by their "origin, customs, languages, and laws."[3] Well into the
modern period, language competed with other criteria to define
nations. Humanist discourse north of the Alps, marked both by
a reappropriation of Greek and Roman ethnographic discourse
and the rediscovery in the late fifteenth century of Tacitus's *Germania*, developed a vision of a German nation existing across
time as a community of descent, characterized by a unique
cultural tradition and a sense of honor that distinguished it in
particular from the Germans' French and Italian neighbors and
rivals.[4] Tacitus, however, says nothing of a Germanic language,
and it is certainly not a major distinguishing characteristic of
his *Germani*. In the early modern period the extent and identity
of this Germanic nation remained uncertain and contradictory:
Within a multiethnic empire headed by an elected emperor, the
concept of German identity was often tied to German defense
of the imperial office against French and English claimants and
a defense of German culture against the pretensions of Italian
humanists. Those who embodied Germanic identity did not
necessarily inhabit a defined Germanic region, nor did they
necessarily speak German. This could result, as in the case of
Emperor Charles V (1500–1558), in the election of a monarch
born in Ghent whose power base was in Spain rather than in
German-speaking lands. Nor did the nation necessarily include
all of the population. The German nation itself included primarily the nobility, the elite—who in their freedom and virtue
were the true heirs of the free Germanic peoples of Tacitus,
increasingly identified as the descendants of Charlemagne and

his Franks. The prioritization of language—and the elevation of a particular linguistic tradition to the status of key to the essence of a people or nation including everyone, regardless of social standing, who shared this language—developed only gradually and under the influence not only of German but also of French philosophical reflections.

One of the first to make explicit the identity between language and national character was the French philosopher Étienne Bonnot de Condillac (1714–80). Condillac's argument, that "each language expresses the character of the people who speak it," was developed not within the kind of nationalist discourses that would develop in Germany but rather within what would be considered a deeply classicizing discourse.[5] In the second book of his *Essai sur l'origine des connaissances humaines* (1746), he argues that "two things compete to form the character of peoples, climate and government."[6] This is a tradition inherited from classical antiquity. He was by no means arguing that this character is unchanging and unchangeable. On the contrary, he was arguing that the character of peoples changes constantly as long as there is no stability in government. Although climate may predispose a people to one or another form of government, this can be altered by many circumstances, and language will reflect these changes. His examples, too, are classical: Latin, he remarks, in contrast with French, has a larger vocabulary for agriculture than for noble warfare because of the different priorities of the two societies. Moreover, he places no particular importance on the earliest manifestations of languages, especially not of French. He explains "that languages change and that genius can develop in a nation only when its language has begun to have fixed principles and a decided character." "This," he explains, "is why it took us so long before we began to write in the vernacular and why those who first tried to do so could not provide a character appropriate to their style." French prior to the age of Corneille was necessarily primitive because France was unstable, and this instability and barbarity even prevented French people from writing eloquently in Latin: "Indeed, the further back we go in time, the more our language was barbarous and the more we were separated from knowledge of the Latin language. And we did not begin to write well in Latin until we were capable of doing so in French."[7]

A second aspect or observation—which, although almost an aside for Condillac, became a central argument in German Romantic philology—was that while in general he saw the earliest forms of a language as primitive, barbarous, and inadequate, "one must note that in a language that is not formed from the debris of other languages, the progress must be much quicker, because it has a character from its very origin." Condillac, the Jesuit-educated scholar, was of course thinking of Greek, and he adds that "the Greeks had excellent writers from the beginning."[8]

Condillac's reflections on both the way that language reflects national character and on the precociousness of Greek—which, because of its purity, demonstrated this character from the very beginning—had an enormous influence on German Enlightenment thinkers, but in a way that fundamentally changed the French philosopher's intention. German humanism had long looked to Tacitus's *Germania* as a validation of ancient Germanic virtue, finding value in archaism. But since Tacitus had nothing to say about the Germanic language, this tradition had emphasized German freedom, purity, and manly virtue. Johann Gottfried Herder (1744–1803), in his *Über den Ursprung der Sprache*— even while claiming to reject Condillac's understanding of language—actually grafted the French philosopher's linguistic principles onto a moral discourse previously developed by German humanists about the value of the primitive, thus making language a tool of German exceptionalism.[9] Herder embraced

Condillac's notion that "tout confirme donc que chaque langue exprime le caractère du peuple qui la parle," and he took this in an essentializing rather than in a developmental sense. The German language became the principal cultural object through which German identity was to be cultivated, with Herder (in his famous poem "An die Deutschen") admonishing his fellow Germans to "spew out the ugly slime of the Seine."

The Napoleonic wars served to transform the cultural nationalism of Herder into a political nationalism, particularly through the influence of figures such as Johann Gottlieb Fichte (1762–1814), whose political discourse explicitly connected national language and national character. But although this tradition developed most precociously in Germany, across much of Western and Central Europe and beyond, language played a central role in efforts to define nations and identify their members. Nations, increasingly understood as linguistic groups, had a natural right to political autonomy. However, just as language needed reformation and purification, so too did society, so that the authentic members of the nation, speaking their authentic language, could provide the foundation for national unity.

Given this intellectual background, it is hardly surprising that in the eighteenth and nineteenth centuries, scholars assumed that the gradual appearance in the written record of vernacular words, phrases, and—ultimately—whole texts was evidence of the growing self-awareness of Europeans as belonging to separate peoples, peoples who asserted their identity by expressing themselves not in the language of a past imperial power but in their own. But was this actually so? Why, beginning in roughly the eighth century, do Europeans begin for the very first time to put down on parchment languages no doubt long spoken but never before written? Under what circumstances do those who exercise power begin not simply to speak languages other than Latin (which they no doubt had done for centuries) but now to commit these words to writing? Is this indeed the expression of emerging national or ethnic sentiment, or is it something else?

These are the questions that I decided to explore when invited by the Historical Society of Israel to deliver the 2010 Jerusalem Lectures in History in Memory of Menahem Stern, and these chapters are lightly revised versions of these lectures. I wish to express at the outset my gratitude to the Historical Society of Israel for this opportunity to explore with Israeli readers the relationship between language, identity, and power and in so doing to pay tribute to the memory of Menahem Stern, a great historian of antiquity who deserved better than murder at the hands of a terrorist while walking through the Valley of the Cross.

Moreover, the invitation gave me the opportunity to connect yet again with Israeli friends and colleagues whose scholarship and generosity I have long admired. Among these in particular I wish to thank Iris Shagrir and Yitzhak Hen, two scholars whose deep knowledge of Christian religious tradition and ritual place them in the forefront of interpreters of medieval culture and whose kindness to me during my stay in Jerusalem helped me develop a new appreciation for the extraordinarily vibrant community of Israeli medievalists. I am also grateful to Gadi Algazi, with whom my friendship now extends over two decades and who, along with Yitzhak Hen, continues to introduce me to the complex layers of Israeli history and geography, from Masada and Qumran on my previous visit to Israel to the Kinneret cemetery overlooking the Sea of Galilee during my most recent one.

Thus I gladly accepted the opportunity to reflect on issues in a distant past and in distant places in a way that might be meaningful in our common, troubled present.

The subject of these chapters is the long history of the use of vernacular language in the exercise of power between antiquity and the high Middle Ages. In short, I want to explore what using vernacular languages meant in the performance of power between the end of the Roman Empire and the thirteenth century.[10] What did it mean to draw attention not simply to the content of discourse, but especially to the language register in which this discourse was expressed? The relevance of such questions is not by any means restricted to the distant past. Language politics and the instrumentalization of language are very much a part of our contemporary world.

# 1 Inventing the Linguistic Monuments of Europe

No one, whether professional historian or member of the interested public, comes to the Middle Ages without preconceptions, assumptions, and expectations about this long period of European history. These preconceptions derive not only from popular media including film, fiction, and the Internet, but also from centuries of debate and fashioning and refashioning of this long period by scholars who sought not only to understand the past but also to mobilize it for debates about their own presents. The Middle Ages have never been merely academic—the continuing fascination with the medieval world has always had implications for the understanding of the present, a search for those models, paradigms, and structures, both social and mental, that define the present.

Essential to this process has always been the search for those objects and especially those texts generated during this period, and concomitantly the search for how to understand these documents. The two are intimately interconnected: the selection and privileging of specific documents has always been in relationship to the questions historians have asked; and documents, as they are discovered or rediscovered, are made to fit into patterns of meaning by the scholars who have discovered them.

Although the search for medieval texts has been carried on since the sixteenth century for a variety of religious, political, and ideological reasons, the Middle Ages that we study is for better or worse largely a construct of the nineteenth century. Our corpus of sources owes its preservation and publication to the passion of long-forgotten scholars who sought it out because they hoped that it would answer specific questions about the past and the present, and subsequent generations of scholars and the general public have largely accepted both the scholars' questions and their interpretations of the corpus. My primary interest is understanding the distant echoes of the Middle Ages that are found primarily in written texts, but many of these texts, especially those that convey fragments of vernacular, were first discovered, edited, and categorized in the nineteenth century by a complicated network of extraordinary individual philologists, historians, and librarians. Not only did these men (as far as I know, they were all men) discover these texts, but they decided what the texts were and how they should fit into the various master narratives about the distant past and its relationship to the present. Thus these texts come to us not simply as manuscripts or critical editions; they come with a tradition of interpretation that sets the parameters within which they are to be understood—parameters that are seldom really questioned. Thus we cannot appreciate what it meant to use the vernacular in the Middle Ages without understanding the texts' discovery, one might almost say their invention, in the nineteenth century and their appropriation into alternate regimes of historicity.

As we saw in the introduction, intellectuals of the late eighteenth and early nineteenth centuries developed a heightened sense of the importance of language for defining national character. An essential element of this ideology was not only the rejection of languages deemed foreign to the nation—especially French, in the case of Germany—but also Condillac's assertion that some languages, because of their purity, encapsulated a national identity from their beginning. Johann Gottlieb Fichte (1762–1814), in his fourth address to the German nation, took this argument, which Condillac had applied to classical Greek, and applied it instead to German, arguing that the Germans alone of the "neo-Europeans" remained in the original dwelling place of their ancestral stock and retained their original language, a language that united the German people and put them in direct contact with each other and with the divine in a way that peoples such as the French, which had adopted Latinized languages, could not hope to achieve.[1] Thus, although for Condillac, a language developed and improved as the population that spoke it matured in character, for the German Romantic nationalists, the finest forms of character were fixed in the earliest expressions of a national language.

Thus by the early nineteenth century, language and identity were increasingly viewed as inseparable, and the most primitive forms of languages as those that displayed most clearly the essences of separate peoples. Shorn of Condillac's developmental schema, the search for archaic origins, rather than the continuous striving for perfection, became the goal of philology.

Not surprisingly, then, philologists turned to the discovery and examination of the earliest vernacular texts in order to discover the first and purest records of national consciousness and identity. This search was by no means limited to German philologists: the assumption that the earliest monuments of language could be instructive for the present was widely held. However, just how these texts might contribute to the construction of the present differed widely according to national culture and individual interest. Nor were all of the philologists and archivists who discovered or edited these texts motivated by a search for monuments of national identity: whatever uses their texts were put to by their contemporaries, the actual researchers who scoured Europe's libraries and archives for ancient texts did so out of a variety of motivations. Although some were indeed on personal quests to find texts that would glorify their national heritage, others were traditional philologists who were simply passionate about linguistic research, and still others were in the service of governments looking for evidence in territorial or political disputes. Scholars seeking out the earliest linguistic records of European languages undertook their research, as we do, for a wide spectrum of personal, institutional, and political reasons. However, in the atmosphere of competitive nationalism and Romantic notions of philological authenticity, the texts that they discovered, edited, and created are the corpus of texts that today we have come to accept as forming the core of national literatures and linguistic heritages.

The first decades of the nineteenth century were a period of extraordinary discoveries for European philologists. At the same time that Indo-European philology was making enormous strides and transforming the understanding of languages and their relationship to each other and to contemporary European civilization, the combination of the secularization of ancient monasteries, dislocations caused by the Napoleonic conquests, and the growing professionalism of philology led to major discoveries of long-lost or ignored medieval texts across Europe.[2] In the spirit of nineteenth-century cultural and political nationalism, it was insufficient, however, simply to discover, edit, comment, and translate these texts. They had to be assigned to national cultures and languages so that they could become part of wider political and cultural programs of rights and claims— not about the pasts in which they were produced, but about the present in which they were found.

In the past decade or so, numerous detailed studies have appeared, studies that chronicle the processes by which philologists made such contributions to a wide spectrum of national cultural projects. This chapter, while drawing on a number of these case studies, seeks to reflect on some of the less obvious aspects of this process. Its case studies suggest something of the range of motivations and traditions that, collectively, led to the creation of the corpus of medieval vernacular texts.

Identifying and claiming these vernacular language texts for specific national traditions was seldom simple or straightforward. As Joep Leerssen has pointed out, these texts, elevated to the classics of "national" traditions, emerged as such only in the process of serious contestation between competing scholars and interpretative traditions.[3] Many of the texts were discovered—and, indeed, produced—outside of the geographical boundaries of the nations that sought to claim them as their own cultural heritage. The languages in which the texts were written were often not easily or unambiguously connected to modern national languages. Moreover, not only were these texts often claimed by more than one national tradition, but the national schools themselves were at the same time just beginning to be defined in an equally complex and competing process in which these discoveries became the medium through which conflicts were conducted.

Finally, one of the ironies of the entire process is that although individual scholars were searching and claiming these newly discovered manuscripts for their particularist national traditions, the scholars themselves were linked by personal contacts, similar experiences, and webs of correspondence on a truly continental scope. They often shared similar educational backgrounds. A good number had met in Paris at the end of the Napoleonic wars, as members of delegations sent to recover manuscripts taken as booty by the French.[4] Many others exchanged letters with each other concerning their discoveries and read the publications of scholars in other national and linguistic fields. The search for individual national identities was, then, paradoxically one of the most international cultural pursuits of the early nineteenth century.

Why such collaborative, international activities ultimately reinforced divisions rather than reducing them must be explained not so much in the content of the manuscripts uncovered from Italy to Scandinavia, but in the context of the competing ideological and cultural values of the scholars who discovered and published them. These discoveries often became the immediate objects of controversy, pitting scholars against each other for reasons at least as much national and personal as scholarly.

Some of these discoveries were made by traditional philologists. Classical scholars such as the Italian Angelo Mai (1782–1854) continued to discover not only long-lost texts by ancient authors but vernacular texts as well.[5] The most famous of these episodes for English speakers was that which resulted from the first publication of *Beowulf* in 1815 by the Danish Icelander Grímur Jónsson Thorkelín (1752–1829), an event that immediately became part of Danish and German ideological arguments concerning Schleswig-Holstein.[6] In the East, Jernej Kopitar (1780–1844) made important manuscript discoveries and editions, most significantly publishing the first fully annotated edition of the so-called Freising Fragments, which came into the Bavarian Royal Library with the secularizations carried out at the start of the nineteenth century.[7] In Germany, a number of nationally inspired philologists such as Eberhard Graff (1780–1841)[8] and Hans Ferdinand Massmann (1797–1874)[9] traveled throughout Europe, uncovering and editing vernacular-language texts that they believed formed the foundation of German culture and identity. In England, the French philologist Francisque Michel (1809–87) scoured British libraries for medieval French texts.[10]

With the possible exception of Kopitar, none of these men are remembered today as among the great philologists of the nineteenth century. Certainly none were in the league of the Grimm brothers, Jacob (1785–1863) and Wilhelm (1786–1859). Nor did they, like Karl Lachmann (1793–1851), develop significant new theories of editing. Their contributions were to the discovery and publishing of texts, glosses, and fragments of vernacular rather than to the elaboration of sophisticated rules of Indo-European grammar and language that came to dominate the new philology of the nineteenth century. Nevertheless, in their various domains they, and others like them, created what would be seen as the medieval corpora of their national languages. Their careers, motivations, and publications ultimately created the parameters within which much subsequent European scholarship would be conducted. Today, their editions are generally considered outdated and woefully inadequate; indeed, even at the time that they were published, some were regarded in this light by professionals such as Lachmann. Nevertheless, these scholars remain, in the macabre but all too accurate phrase of Stephan Müller, *"Untote,"* the "living dead"—scholars whose all-but-forgotten work continues to influence not only philology but our very understanding of the past that they sought to resurrect.[11]

The activities of some of these scholars developed out of earlier traditions of religious and national scholarship already well established in the eighteenth century. The career of the Italian classicist and librarian Angelo Mai, for example, developed in the tradition of classically trained, humanistic ecclesiastics of centuries before him, but the new circumstances of library consolidations as well as new technologies of research permitted him to make discoveries that electrified the world of learning.

Mai, a Jesuit and a classics teacher in Naples, was appointed in 1811 to a position in the venerable Biblioteca Ambrosiana in Milan, founded by Cardinal Federico Borromeo (1564–1631). The Ambrosiana contained over 15,000 manuscripts, including most of the collection of the monastery of Bobbio, which—before its dissolution in 1803—had housed some of the most ancient manuscripts in Europe. Mai, who became the librarian of the Ambrosiana in 1813, was not only a gifted Latinist but also an excellent paleographer. Working through the manuscripts of Bobbio, he made discovery after discovery of fragmentary manuscripts of ancient classical texts that monks had reused for writing Christian texts.

Mai belonged both to the tradition of classical scholarship and to the world of nineteenth-century science. His success in deciphering ancient manuscripts was the result of technology as well as of philology. His methods for reading palimpsests depended on chemical technology, methods that were disputed even in his own day. He often treated manuscripts with a tincture of oak gall to bring out the underlying text. He found that even where the original writing had been scraped from the parchment so that it was almost invisible, enough ink remained that when the leaf was soaked in a tannic acid solution made from the gall, blue or red outlines of the writing reappeared. The technique may have permitted a momentary darkening of the original text so that he could transcribe it, but it could also result in the ultimate darkening of the manuscript leaf so that it was rendered permanently illegible. Nevertheless, one could not dispute the importance of the discoveries he made by this methodology, which included fragments of Cicero's orations and the correspondence of Fronto. In 1819 Mai left the Jesuit order and assumed similar responsibilities at the Bibliotheca Vaticana. There he continued to make important discoveries, the most significant of which was a palimpsest of lost portions of Cicero's *De re publica*, which Mai published in 1822. Nor were his finds restricted to ancient Latin texts. He discovered and published Greek texts, including previously unknown portions of Dionysius of Halicarnassus's *Roman Antiquities* and an oration by Isaeus. Mai's discoveries and publications—which regularly appeared in his series *Scriptorum veterum nova collectio* (1825–38), *Spicilegium Romanum* (1839–44), and *Patrum nova collectio* (1852–54)—won widespread admiration and the envy of scholars across Europe.[12]

Although Mai's greatest achievements were in the area of Latin and Greek manuscripts, in 1817 he made an announcement that caught the attention—indeed, roused the passion—of German philologists. Among the palimpsests that he had discovered from the Bobbio manuscripts in the Ambrosiana and Vatican libraries were pages of the Wulfila's Gothic translation of the Bible, as well as portions of a hitherto unknown commentary in Gothic on the Gospel of John.[13] The interest in this discovery was intense among national language scholars who already considered Gothic the earliest written form of German and imagined the Goths to be their own ancestors. Mai wanted to be the one to publish these texts and consequently would not permit anyone to see the new fragments. However, in spite of his great learning, Mai was no Germanicist, and he ultimately entrusted the work to the Italian orientalist and philologist Count Carlo Ottavio Castiglione (1784–1849)—who was a fine scholar but also had little knowledge of Gothic. Castiglione published a very problematic edition of one page of the manuscript in 1819, but years passed with no publication of the remainder of these Gothic texts.

Grímur Thorkelín's decision to travel to England in search of manuscripts was likewise within the context of a long-established tradition. Since the seventeenth century, Icelanders had made their way to Copenhagen for education and professional advancement and had found that their native language, with its very close relationship to Old Norse, made them ideal collectors, editors, and guardians of Old Norse texts. The most famous of these Icelanders was Árni Magnússon (1663–1730). As secretary of the Royal Danish Archives, he traveled extensively in Iceland, discovering and acquiring surviving manuscripts in Old Norse. He brought them back to Copenhagen, where they became Den Arnamagnæanske Håndskriftsamling, the most important collection of old Norse manuscripts and papers in the world.[14] Although Árni seems to have been inspired primarily by a love of Icelandic language and culture, the royal support that he received for his collecting was inspired by political concerns. In Iceland, Árni had found Swedes who were purchasing manuscripts of historical importance, and the Danish state, seeing this as a threat to its claim to represent the continuity of medieval Norse legitimacy, forbade the export of these manuscripts and empowered Árni to collect them for transport to Copenhagen.

In the next generation, the Keeper of the Royal Privy Archives, Jacob Langebek (1710–75), continued Árni's practice of discovering Norse materials and traveled extensively in Scandinavia to copy manuscripts relevant to Danish history, which he subsequently published in the series *Scriptores rerum danicarum medii aevi*. Thorkelín's decision to travel to England to do the same, and the Danish crown's willingness to support him, was thus in keeping with a long-established royal interest in Danish history, an interest directly related to Denmark's imperial program in Iceland and Norway. Moreover, Thorkelín may have been aware of the fact that Humphrey Wanley's catalog of Anglo-Saxon books from 1705 had listed a poem described as "a most noble description of the wars of one Scuylding king Beowulf against Swedish foes."[15] Such a text, particularly given the rivalry between the Danish and Swedish crowns, was an ideal text to bring to the attention of a Danish audience.

In Vienna, Kopitar, like Thorkelín a provincial drawn to an imperial capital for education and then a career, became the leading publisher and scholar of south Slavic linguistic material. Kopitar's early career followed a pattern that was firmly rooted in ancient traditions of patronage and private scholarship. He was from a small village in Carniola, and he had begun his studies in Ljubljana before becoming a private tutor in the home of Baron Sigmund (in Slovenian, Žiga) Zois, the son of a Venetian merchant who had married into a Slovene family. Zois patronized a wide spectrum of writers and intellectuals and became the center of what would later be called the Slovene enlightenment. In 1808 Kopitar published his *Grammatik der slavischen Sprache in Krain, Kärnten und Steyermark* (Grammar of the Slavic Language in Krain, Carinthia and Steyermark), which established his reputation as a philologist.[16] In the same year he moved to Vienna to study law, but instead he became a librarian at the Vienna court's library, where he continued his study of Slavic languages and developed his theory of the ethnic unity of the Slavic-speaking inhabitants of what had been the Illyrian provinces under Napoleon. Kopitar considered Slovenian the most archaic and the closest to Old Church Slavonic, and thus the purest, of all Slavonic languages.

Kopitar's intellectual horizons were not limited to Vienna or the world of Habsburg Slavicists. He corresponded with international scholars such as Jacob Grimm and the great Czech philologist Josef Dobrovský, who shared his interests in philology if not in south Slavic languages. In 1814, Kopitar was sent to Paris as part of an Austrian delegation to reclaim the manuscripts that Napoleon had expropriated from the Austrian imperial library. Kopitar not only successfully completed his mission in Paris, but he also spent time there examining Slavic manuscripts and meeting scholars from across Europe who had similarly been sent to recover manuscripts confiscated by Napoleon. From France, Kopitar traveled to England, where he met with scholars in London and Oxford.[17]

Back in Vienna, which Kopitar hoped could be the capital of a south Slavic intellectual world, he continued to work on the origins and dissemination of the Slavic language, particularly on the origins of Old Church Slavonic. For information about new manuscripts and texts, he relied on his network of scholars. He was aware of the extraordinary finds of long-forgotten manuscripts being made by Angelo Mai and sought to accomplish similar feats for Slavic manuscripts.[18] His interest in Slavic manuscripts led him to two extremely important early texts that aligned neatly with his Habsburg and Catholic interests. The first of these was the *Glagolita Clozianus*, a manuscript containing fragments of homilies by Athanasius of Alexandria, John Chrysostom, Epiphanius of Salamis, and an anonymous homilist whom some identify as Methodius, apostle to the Slavs. The manuscript was written in Glagolitic script in the first third of the eleventh century. For centuries it had been kept in the family of the Frangipani on the island of Krk; in the early nineteenth century, it was acquired by Count Paris Cloz, who donated it to the city library of Trento. The second manuscript was of perhaps even greater importance to Kopitar. This was the Freising Fragments, fragments of an even earlier Slavic text in Latin characters first discovered in 1806 among the manuscripts removed from Freising and taken to the royal library in Munich.[19] In 1814 the great Czech philologist Josef Dobrovský published the first preliminary analysis of these texts.[20] Dobrovský described the manuscript, provided the *incipits* and *excipits* of the texts, and postulated that they originated "in Kärnten, oder Krain, oder gar in Bayern" (in Carinthia, or Carniola, or even in Bavaria). However, he did not publish the texts: "I intentionally abstain from any elucidation which these precious remains certainly merit, because I do not wish to anticipate natives of the Krain, who will not tarry long to make known these ancient monuments of their language and to provide them with an appropriate commentary."[21]

Dobrovský presumably had Kopitar's patron Baron Sigmund Zois in mind when he wrote these generous lines, but neither

Zois nor any other south Slavic scholar immediately took up the task.[22] Ultimately the task fell to Kopitar, he needed twenty-five years before he published his edition of the three Slavic fragments.[23] Instead, the first edition appeared six years later, edited not by a south Slav but by two scholars from a very different— and, for the Catholic Habsburg Kopitar, problematic—pole of the Slavic world: Moscow.[24] The first scholar was Petr Ivanovich Köppen, grandson of a German who became physician to the Tsar and son of a well-respected geographer and ethnographer of Russian culture. The second was Alexandr Khristoforovich Vostokov, an illegitimate son of Baron von Osten-Sacken, an imperial officer originally from what is now Tallin. Vostokov became the foremost Slavic philologist in Russia.[25] Both of these men, but especially Vostokov, were deeply interested in the history of Slavic languages and the relationship between the language of early texts such as the Freising Fragments and the debates over the relative influence of Eastern Christian traditions—supposedly represented by Cyril and Methodius—on the one hand and Western Christian traditions emanating from Germany on the other hand. Nor surprisingly, Vostokov and Köppen argued that the fragments were related to the "Carniolan" language of the tenth century, closely related to Old Church Slavonic.[26] However, they saw the origins of Old Church Slavonic as an Eastern Christian tradition closely related to Orthodoxy. Although Vostokov acknowledged that the language of the texts was related to modern Serbian or Croatian, the suggestion that these texts were related to Old Church Slavonic, thus connecting them to an Eastern rather than a Western tradition, was at odds with the Catholic Slavic tradition espoused by Kopitar and his Viennese Slovenian circle.

If Mai, Thorkelín, and Kopitar developed their knowledge and philological activities out of the paradigms of previous centuries, the Germans Graff and especially Massmann belonged to a new and quite different world of Romantic German nationalism, at the center of which lay philology. Graff was a native of Elbing (today Elbląg, in Poland) where, after studying at the University of Königsberg (modern Kaliningrad), he became a Gymnasium teacher and educational administrator. After holding various administrative positions, he served on the administrative council under the Freiherr von Stein and became a theorist of educational reform.

However, his life was transformed by his encounters with Jacob Grimm's 1819 *Deutsche Grammatik* and by his acquaintance, in his capacity as an educator, with Karl Lachmann, who in 1818 became professor *extraordinarius* of classical philology at the University of Königsberg. Lachmann lectured both on classical philology and on Old High German, lectures that Graff eagerly followed. The twin influences of Grimm and Lachmann on the Gymnasium teacher were enormous. Grimm had listed among the desiderata of Germanic philology a complete glossary of Old High German words, but neither Grimm nor Lachmann was personally interested in compiling such a list. Graff, who had been collecting Old High German words on his own for some time, immediately took up the challenge. Five years later, with the support of Lachmann and Grimm, he produced a study of Old High German prepositions that won him a professorship in Königsberg, a position that allowed him to travel extensively in Germany, Switzerland, France, and Italy, searching for manuscripts containing Old High German glosses and texts. The first results of these travels appeared in a three-volume work titled *Diutiska*.[27] The volumes were a hodgepodge of newly discovered or reedited texts, glossaries, and the like, but they were introduced by Graff's own poetry and odd bits of material, a reflection of a chaotic approach to his task that would be even more pronounced in his magnum opus, the six-volume *Althochdeutsche Sprachschatz*.[28]

Grimm and Lachmann had wanted a complete collection of the vocabulary of Old High German. This Graff provided, but in an extraordinary and virtually unusable form. Fascinated by the relationship between Sanskrit and German, he rejected the simple idea of organizing this massive material alphabetically or by word stems, which would have been Grimm's preference. Instead, Graff decided to organize the entire collection according to what he assumed to be the Sanskrit roots of the individual entries. Moreover, he organized these in turn not alphabetically but phonetically. The result was an indispensable but unusable monument to Graff's erudition and eccentricity. This strange collection became usable only with the addition of a seventh volume, an alphabetical index, created by an even more extraordinary figure in the history of German Romantic philology, Hans Ferdinand Massmann.

From the age of thirteen, Massmann was an enthusiastic follower of Friedrich Ludwig Jahn (1778–1852). "Turnvater Jahn," as he was widely known, founded gymnastics associations that were intended to restore the moral and physical strength of the German youth. His populist activities, support of *altdeutsche* language and culture, and liberal political ideology made him both a powerful popular figure and a perceived danger to the Prussian state. Massmann became a devoted member of Jahn's circle, although he was too young to join Jahn's Lützow Free Corps to fight the French in the Napoleonic wars. By sixteen, Massmann was composing patriotic verse and corresponding with the members of the corps. During the Hundred Days, he briefly joined the group as a volunteer, but Napoleon's defeat at Waterloo ended hostilities before he and his fellows saw any action. His unit did march to Paris, however, and there he met other patriots—including Karl Müller, who in turn introduced him to Jacob Grimm and the group of scholars who were in Paris to recover plundered manuscripts.[29] After the Napoleonic wars, Massmann combined his gymnastics, political ideology, and study of German philology. He wrote pamphlets and poetry and played a central role in Jahn's efforts to develop an alternative educational system in Prussia and elsewhere around gymnastics, a program that was increasingly seen as *geistiges Turnen*, or intellectual gymnastics. Massmann saw the gymnastics movement as intimately connected to a constitutional movement to unite Germans under a *Turnmeister*, who would protect the freedom of the community. The ideal, he suggested, would be "if the German Kaiser were himself our praiseworthy Turnmeister, as once were Henry the Fowler, Maximilian the First and the other emperors who were the protectors of the bodily art."[30]

In 1816 Jahn moved from Berlin to Jena to establish a gymnastics center at the university. There, the gymnastics movement began to merge with the *Burschenschaft* movement to create a new synthesis of *Burschenturner*.[31] Massmann also traveled widely in Germany as a gymnastics missionary, before returning to Berlin. However, in 1817 the movement and Massmann in particular went too far for governmental authorities when they organized a large assembly of *Burschenturner* at the Wartburg castle in Eisenach—which, because of its association with Martin Luther, who had been given refuge there by the Elector Frederick the Wise following Luther's refusal to recant at the Diet of Worms, had become a symbol of German national identity—on the 18th and 19th of October. Initially, in spite of the anxieties of the Hanover government at the prospect of a great number of students assembling at the Wartburg, the Grand Duke Carl August welcomed them, providing wood for their bonfire and encouraging the local community to provide them with accommodations. However Massmann seized the opportunity to organize a book burning of *"undeutscher* and *turnfeindlicher"* books modeled on Luther's burning of the papal bull of excommunication in 1520—although, as Joachim Burkhard Richter points out, it actually was more similar to the burning of forbidden books by the Inquisition.[32] The burned books included works by collaborators during the Napoleonic occupation, the Code Napoleon, and Saul Ascher's *Germanomanie*. Both the book burning and Massmann's enthusiastic description of it, which he published in the same year, brought him into trouble with the Prussian authorities.[33] Threatened with legal proceedings, he moved to Jena but was pursued by his opponents and ultimately convicted of defaming Wilhelm Scherer, whose book had been burned. However, the penalty, eight days in jail, was only symbolic. By the next year, Massmann had returned to his studies of Germanic philology and, as he wrote to the brothers Grimm in 1818, had decided to dedicate his research and life to "the mother language and the lore of the fatherland in the widest sense of Germanism."[34]

Massmann's dedication to *Germanenthum* was matched by his polemical style and his extreme polemical and political radicalism. He carried on academic feuds with other scholars such as Heinrich Hoffmann and never won the trust or approval of Lachmann.[35] When Massmann learned of the unedited fragments of the Gothic Bible discovered by Mai, he attempted to secure financing from the Berlinische Gesellschaft für deutsche Sprache to travel to Italy, but the Prussian foreign ministry opposed him because of his radicalism, and his funding fell through.[36] Likewise, his radical background led the Freiherr von Stein, founder of the Gesellschaft für ältere deutsche Geschichtskunde, to reject his bid to edit the *Kaiserchronik* for the Monumenta Germaniae Historica.[37] Unable to find a position in Prussia because of his politics, Massmann eventually managed to impress King Ludwig I of Bavaria with his knowledge of the

*Nibelungenlied*, which led in 1830 to a position teaching the Bavarian cadet corps gymnastics and lecturing on Germanic topics at Ludwig Maximilian University.

Massmann had retained his interest in Gothic, which he saw as the origin of the German language, and he hoped to publish the long-announced but still unedited materials that Angelo Mai had discovered in Milan and Rome. In 1833 Massmann obtained a three-month leave from Munich to accompany the crown prince to Italy and to edit the Gothic fragments. But by then, Castiglione had published the first of a series of the Gothic fragments. Massmann wrote a vicious review of the edition, which was rejected for publication in the *Wiener Jarhbücher* by no less a figure than Kopitar.[38] Frustrated that the only remaining Gothic texts that he could edit were the fragments of an anonymous commentary on the Gospel of John, Wassmann nevertheless published an edition of them in 1834 under a grandiloquent title—after the Gothic title "Skeireins aiwaggeljons þairh Johannan," the English title is "The Exegesis of the Gospel of John in the Gothic Language from Roman and Milanese Manuscripts along with a Latin Translation, Accompanying Notes, Historical Investigation, Gothic-Latin Dictionary and Writing Samples. On Behalf of His Royal Highness the Crown Prince Maximilian of Bavaria, Described and Published for the First Time."[39] The text is commonly known as *Skeireins*. In his dedication to the Bavarian king, Massmann emphasized the significance of the text particularly to Bavaria: "Germany, and especially Bavaria and southern Germany, on account of the kinship of dialects, deserves to bring at last to the light of day in a dignified and scientifically complete form the most ancient monuments of its original language, that of the Gothic Bible exegesis of the fourth to sixth centuries, finally united into a whole."[40]

One must acknowledge the tremendous effort that Massmann made to transcribe the palimpsests and to make sense of them. Still, the text itself must have been something of a disappointment to him. Although it was the longest Gothic text after Wulfila's Bible translation, Massmann recognized that it was not an original composition by a Goth but a translation of a Greek text, presumably by the fourth-century Bishop Theodor of Herakleia. Still, in Massmann's long commentary, he emphasized the superiority of the Goths over the "degenerate" Romans as well as their cultural autonomy: "Conquerors and conquered might have easily mixed together; but not so the morally strong Germans with the degenerate Romans. The 'Arian' Goths received and developed their independent national life in Greece and in Italy; they mixed neither customs nor language."[41] In Massmann's hands, the translation of this Greek commentary becomes evidence of German superiority.

In 1833, the same year that Massmann was rushing to compete his edition of *Skeireins*, Francisque Michel, then a young French Romantic and part-time transcriber of medieval manuscripts, set sail for England in the hope of finding manuscripts of value to French history.[42] In some ways, Michel's mission resembled that of Thorkelín, two generations earlier. Both were on officially sponsored research trips, undertaken to discover documents of importance to their nation's history. However, Michel belonged to a very different world than Thorkelín's. Michel was no government servant or fanatic nationalist, but an independent man of letters in love with the Middle Ages, trying to make his way in Paris. The son of a schoolteacher in Lyons, he had joined the circle of Charles Nodier, the leading figure in the French Romantic movement, and through this association had met Victor Hugo, Alexandre Dumas, Emile Deschamps, Alfred de Vigny, and other figures in the French world of letters. Michel even tried his hand at writing, publishing a series of stories in a florid and rather unsuccessful imitation of Sir Walter Scott. However, Michel's romantic engagement with the Middle Ages was much more than that of a dilettante writer of Gothic fiction. He was a passionate reader and editor of medieval French literature, earning his living in Paris by transcribing medieval romances in the Bibliothèque Royale and republishing and even making new editions of texts. He also began to acquire professional paleographical skills by frequenting the lectures at the École Nationale des Chartes, which had been established in 1821 to train a cadre of specialists in the technical study of archival materials. Although he failed to win a scholarship to the École (ranking tenth in a competition for eight positions), he was allowed to continue to participate in the course and became an enthusiastic editor and publisher of Old French texts.

By 1833 Michel had published six Old French texts. He had established enough of a reputation in the small circle of scholars interested in the recovery of such texts that he could write to François Guizot, minister of public instruction and himself a major figure in early medieval historical writing in France, to offer to undertake an expedition to England for the purpose of investigating manuscripts in the libraries of England and Scotland that might be of interest for the study of French literature and history of the Middle Ages.

Guizot (1787–1874), like his contemporary the Prussian Freiherr von Stein (1757–1831), combined a passion for scholarship with his responsibilities for state-sponsored education and— again like Stein, the founder of the Monumenta Germaniae Historica—worked to bring about the editing of those medieval sources that would establish French historical traditions and rights.[43] After checking Michel's credentials, Guizot agreed to arrange a small stipend for him and sent the young scholar off to England with the assignment of copying two manuscripts whose contents bore particularly on the relationship between England and France in the Middle Ages: the *Estoire des Engleis* of Geoffrey Gaimar and the *Chronique des Ducs de Normandie* of Benoît de Sainte-Maure. In London, Michel diligently went about his assigned task, and it was only after a year that he managed to travel to Oxford, where his real quarry lay. In 1775 an English editor of Chaucer had cited several lines from a French manuscript at Oxford that told the story of the hero Roland, an epic story well known in France but extant only in very late versions.[44] Michel was also aware of the work of Gervais de la Rue, who for his *Essais historiques sur les bardes, les jongleurs et les trouvères normands et anglo-normands* had probably examined the manuscript in Oxford.[45] From the start, Michel had recognized that this could well be the lost, authentic version of the *Chanson de Roland*.

By the 1830s, then, across Europe a disparate group of manuscript enthusiasts, for a wide spectrum of reasons, had begun to edit texts ranging from major epics (*Beowulf*, the *Chanson de Roland*) to obscure treatises (*Skeireins*, the Freising Fragments) and anonymous glosses and marginalia. Each man was eager to recover vernacular texts of his own national tradition: Thorkelín sought Danish manuscripts and found *Beowulf*; Kopitar sought Slovenian texts and found the Freising Fragments; Massmann sought German texts and found a Gothic commentary on John; and Michel, searching in Oxford for French historical texts, found the *Chanson de Roland* in Oxford University's Bodleian Library Manuscript Digby 23. But each text presented obstacles to its discoverer's mission.

Thorkelín, whose long-delayed edition of *Beowulf* appeared in 1815, encountered perhaps the worst problems. He pronounced the text to be a *Poema Danicum Dialecto Anglosaxonica*, implying that Anglo-Saxon was a dialect of Old Norse, the ancestral language of the Danish. This in turn implied, as Tom Shippey points out, that not only were the English really Scandinavians "but that their homeland of Angeln, in Slesvig, had also been Scandinavian and should remain so."[46] Jacob Grimm had previously classified Old English as West Germanic rather than Scandinavian, and thus, not surprisingly, the language and origins of *Beowulf* became quickly embroiled in the Schleswig-Holstein controversy. Supporters of the German position, such as Nicholaus Outzen and Friedrich Christoph Dahlmann, argued that the poem was not in a Scandinavian dialect but rather in a Low German branch of West Germanic, evidence that Northern Schleswig was *urdeutsch* and that the Danes had taken it over only after the emigration of the Angles to Britain.[47] The controversy became increasingly heated in subsequent decades, as the territorial dispute erupted into violence. The political issue was ultimately settled not by philology but by Bismarck and the Second Schleswig War. The only group that showed no initial interest in *Beowulf* at all appears to have been the English, who did not adopt the text as part of a national literature for several decades.

By the time Kopitar had published his texts as Old Slovenian, they had already been identified as Old Church Slavonic by his Russian competition. Honoring Vostokov's earlier publication, Kopitar presented the text in four columns: the first a transcription of the manuscript; the second, his rendering into the Slavic orthography that he favored; the third, Vostokov's Cyrillic transliteration; and the fourth, a translation into Latin.[48] However, his interpretation of the text and its meaning differed greatly from that of the Russians. Based on his study of the Freising Fragments and the *Glagolita Clozianus*, Kopitar argued that Karantanija (the ancient region of Pannonia) was the original homeland of Old Church Slavonic, which was essentially Old Slovenian. He also maintained that the Christianization of the Slavs had proceeded from this Western, Latin region rather than from an Orthodox missionary program.[49]

Michel's text also presented problems in terms of national identity. Why, after all, was it preserved in England rather than in France, and in a manuscript betraying elements of Anglo-Norman dialect rather than in pure "Francien"?[50] Was it indeed a French national epic? The year after Michel's first publication of the manuscript, Wilhelm Grimm, in his edition of the Middle High German *Ruolandes Liet*, reviewed all of the known versions of the Roland story, including Michel's newly published Digby 23 text, and then argued: *"The Song of Roland*, in which the German names of the heroes are still partly preserved, may well have been sung in the earliest time in the Frankish language, and only after its disappearance, devolved exclusively into Romance poetry. Rightly did [Ludwig] Uhland express the view that in the strict gravity and in the in the coarseness of the Frankish heroic the German spirit from which they emerged, still shines through."[51]

Michel, while fully aware of the importance of his discovery for French culture, was not particularly interested in debates of national identity. A philologist and enthusiast of medieval texts generally, his intellectual activities were far from nationalist in scope. For example, in the same year that he published the *Chanson de Roland*, he also published a catalog of publications on Anglo-Saxon compiled from the libraries of Oxford and Cambridge Universities,[52] as well as an anonymous Anglo-Norman poem on the conquest of Ireland[53]—neither of which were part of his commission from Guizot. With the *Chanson de Roland*, he was less concerned with its national character than with understanding several points. First, why, according to the twelfth-century *Roman de Rou*, did a Norman *trouvère* named Taillefer supposedly sing at the battle of Hastings "de Karlemaigne e de Rollant, / e d'Oliver e des vassals / qui morurent en Rencesvals" (Of Charlemagne and of Roland, and of Oliver and the vassals who died at Roncesvalles)?[54] Second, was the Digby text what Taillefer sang? Michel believed that he had found his answer to the first question in lines 372–73 of *Chanson de Roland*, in which Blandandrin speaks of Charlemagne's journey "across the salt sea" to win for Saint Peter his tribute.[55] In his excited letter to Claude Fauriel announcing his discovery, Michel explained that "you see that the Norman trouvère, author or arranger of the poem, established a precedent in favor of William the Conqueror, who was going to conquer England in the shadow of the standard of Saint Peter."[56] His response to the second question was affirmative, arguing that Taillefer's song was surely taken from a *chanson de geste*, and that this mention of fighting in England under the banner of Saint Peter as well as the antiquity of the language—which Michel considered the same as that used in the laws of William the Conqueror—was evidence that Turold's poem and that of Taillefer were the same.[57]

If Michel was not particularly interested in the national implications of his poem, neither was his patron Guizot—initially. After his return to France, Michel requested that his edition be published by the Imprimerie Royale, but his request was refused, and he had to publish the work at his own expense in a printing of just 200 copies.[58] Only after its appearance was it hailed by others such as Xavier Marmier, who called it "peut-être notre plus ancienne, notre véritable épopée nationale" in his review in *Le Monde*.[59]

If Michel was more interested in the historical than the national implications of his discovery, Massmann was quite the opposite. His whole purpose in publishing the *Skeireins* was to glorify the German people through this monument of their language. But this text may have had been the one with the weakest connection to a nation or people. A text written by a Greek ecclesiastic and then translated, perhaps in Constantinople, for a society in an unknown location was a shaky foundation on which to construct a theory of Germanic—let alone specifically German—cultural superiority, but such was Massmann's goal.

What can we conclude about the work of these "living dead" in terms of their own times and ours? First, we recognize that although they came from widely different parts of Europe, they belonged to a society of letters that drew them into frequent personal and literary contact with each other. Nor was this always a matter of national rivalry, as would be the case later in the century. If Danish and German scholars immediately saw the possible political implications of *Beowulf*, and if Russian and Habsburg philologists saw the importance of disputing the language of the Freising Fragments, for the most part they did not see their pursuit of the monuments of their particular national traditions to be exclusive or—perhaps with the exception of Massmann—necessarily antagonistic. Kopitar maintained a long and lively contact with Germanic philologists, especially Jacob Grimm, who indeed was the central node for communication about all vernacular philology, editions, and folklore regardless of language. Michel worked closely with English scholars such as Thomas Wright and John Kemble and later published not only on Old French but also English, Scottish, Spanish, and even Basque literature and texts.[60]

The second conclusion concerning the success of these early scholars in claiming their vernacular texts for their national traditions is more complex. Is *Beowulf* Danish or German, or is it a monument of Anglo-Saxon culture? Is the *Chanson de Roland* a French national epic? Is *Skeireins* a monument of German language? Are the Freising Fragments the earliest record of Slovenian? These questions, first posed by this pioneering generation of philologists, have cast a long shadow across not simply European philology but European history. In the course of the nineteenth and twentieth centuries, these texts would continue to be claimed as essential elements in the elaboration of competing national pasts. But do these arguments make historical sense today?

About the only thing that philologists seem to be able to agree on concerning the date and composition of *Beowulf* is that it is entirely irrelevant to the issues of Danish and German identity politics to which Thorkelín and his opponents attempted to apply it. The date of its composition still ranges between the seventh and eleventh centuries; why this poem, which never mentions England and which takes place in what are today southern Sweden and Denmark, should have been composed in Anglo-Saxon is unclear; and virtually every other contextual issue continues to be debated.[61] The question of whether *Skeireins* is merely a translation of Theodor or an original Gothic compilation drawing on Theodor as well as other Greek patristic texts continues to be discussed, but the consensus today is that the commentary is indeed a translation and as such belongs to the world of fourth-century Greek patristic literature and has no connection with the *Völkerwanderungszeit*.[62] The *Song of Roland* in Digby 23 is indeed a French-language text, but it is equally an English one, evidence of the transnational culture of the Anglo-Norman elite of the twelfth century. And finally the Freising Fragments, even today venerated in the young republic of Slovenia as the foundational documents of the Slovenian language,[63] are being reassessed, not as texts in early Slovenian but as items prepared for a now long-disappeared Alpine Slavic community somewhere considerably to the west of Slovenia and even Carinthia. In the final analysis, Dobrovský may have been right in his early suggestion that these monuments of "Slovenian" may actually have been intended for a community in Bavaria.

In suggesting that the ways in which these early texts were first brought to light and appreciated may have set their analysis on courses that have been more a distraction than a help should in no way detract from the extraordinary scholarship of their discoverers. Although others worked out theoretical frameworks of Indo-European philology, these scholars provided the raw material for all subsequent studies of early European vernaculars, and they did so largely without the grammars, dictionaries, and other apparatus that could be created only simultaneously with the appearance of these texts. The fact that their efforts were part of wider political and ideological programs inevitably influenced their results, and it takes nothing away from their achievement, even if we must understand these often forgotten intellectual horizons so that we do not allow the nationalist ghosts of these living dead to haunt the present.

# 2 Religion and Language

The previous chapter examined the rediscovery in the nineteenth century of the vernacular heritage of the Middle Ages. My purpose was to suggest that vernacular texts of the Middle Ages, in spite of the interest in them by philologists and historians looking for national origins and ethnic expressions, were anything but prima facie expressions of national or ethnic communities. Their relationships to the communities that claimed them in the nineteenth century were complex and contradictory, their origins and original purpose anything but evident. But if the development of written vernacular was not the result of the development of national cultures, what was it? In this chapter and the next one, I will look at two faces of the development of the vernacular within the exercise of power. The first is vernacular language and sacred power. The second will reflect on vernacular language and secular power.

If Christianity, unlike Islam or Judaism, lacks a sacred language, how did Latin become in effect a sacred language for the Western Church? The answer is not as straightforward as one might think.

As it did in many other spheres, Christianity introduced a revolution of values within language acquisition and use, even though its greatest proponents were among the most highly educated Christians of the late fourth and early fifth centuries, specifically Jerome and Augustine.

Christianity presented a double paradox: First, by laying claim to Jewish sacred scriptures written in Hebrew and Aramaic, Roman Christians acknowledged the significance of texts written in neither of the high-status languages of antiquity. Second, as Erich Auerbach pointed out long ago, the imperative to preach the gospel to all in a language that they could understand, as well as the humble style of these very texts, brought about a transformation in Christian attitudes toward Latin style even among Latin-speaking Christians.[1]

Although earlier generations of Christians made do with the Septuagint, which at least had the merit of being in Greek, and Western Christians created Latin translations of this text, Jerome, the first and perhaps the only serious philologist of nonclassical languages in the history of Rome, took the radical step of learning Hebrew and Aramaic or Syriac in order to retranslate scripture from its original languages.[2] Augustine was not particularly enthusiastic about Jerome's retranslation project, but he had his own interest in nonclassical languages, specifically Punic. This Roman rhetorician acknowledged having learned Punic from his nurse, although he was raised and educated entirely in Latin. Nevertheless he found himself the staunch defender of Punic in his polemical letter addressed to Maximus of Madaura, in which he castigated his opponent for mocking the vernacular language of North Africa: "Nor can you have so forgotten yourself, given that you are an African man writing in Africa, that we are both settled in Africa, that you would deem Punic names worthy of censure. . . . If this language is rejected by you, deny what has been asserted by many wise men, namely that much wisdom has been preserved in Punic books. You should regret having been born here, where the cradle of this language is still warm."[3]

In his letter to Maximus, Augustine was attempting to score rhetorical points against his opponent, so his defense of Punic might here be regarded with skepticism. Elsewhere, however, he is more unambiguously supportive of the Punic language, in particular deciding—in the appointment of a bishop of Fussala, a small *castellum* near the border of what is now Tunisia and Algeria—to insist that the individual be instructed in the Punic language.[4] The important point here is not simply Augustine's respect for the abstract value of the Punic language or, as some have suggested, his recognition that Punic was related to Hebrew, the language of the Bible. Rather, it is his very real fear that, in the competition between orthodoxy and Donatism, knowledge of the local vernacular was essential. From this perspective, the local vernacular was not to be learned or appreciated for its intrinsic value, but instead because it was likely to be the vehicle of heterodoxy and thus also the best way to combat it.

This is perhaps a variant of the traditional Roman disdain for languages other than Greek and Latin, but it is tinged with a certain fear. Jerome, at times under suspicion of heterodox beliefs himself, references this same anxiety in his letter to Presbyter Marcus.[5] There he denigrates his own ability in Syriac, but he does so to mock his opponents who believe that he uses his linguistic skills to sow schism: "Clearly you fear lest this man, extremely fluent in Syriac and in Greek, will travel around the churches seducing the people and creating schism."[6]

Often taken as evidence of his poor command of the language, this satirical comment is actually a defense of his own conduct, arguing in effect that his Syriac was not good enough to allow him to spread heresy in it. Thus conceived, popular languages become a battleground between orthodoxy and heterodoxy: knowledge of them is necessary to combat heresy, but it may also be a primary vehicle for heresy. The paradox would endure for centuries.

Along with anxiety concerning the circulation of heresy, Augustine and other orthodox bishops feared the development of erroneous interpretations of scripture on the part of those lacking a proper education. His *De doctrina christiana*, which elaborated the Christian approach to scriptural interpretation that would dominate Western Christendom for over a millennium, begins with a frontal assault on those who assert that they could read and interpret scripture without the benefit of formal direction or education but simply through direct divine inspiration. Mastering the secrets of sacred scripture required proper training, both to understand scripture oneself and to convey this understanding to others. Thus, by the end of antiquity Christianity—unlike other religions of the book, in which the word of God was contained within a specific sacred language—faced a complex dilemma. On the one hand, Christians possessed no sacred language: neither Hebrew nor Greek was the exclusive means of communicating the word of God. Rather, Christian teachers had the obligation to communicate the hidden truths of scripture in a language that people could understand. But on the other hand, there was a danger that access to the sacred might be the source of heterodoxy, and this danger was even greater if it circulated in languages other than Greek and Latin, languages in which the *accessus* to revealed truth had been elaborated.

In the eastern churches, the development of Coptic and especially Syriac as fully elaborated, written languages into which scripture was translated and, equally important, in which theological commentary and apparatus was developed, appeared quite early: by the seventh century, no fewer than six versions of the scriptures existed in Syriac, from Tatian's *Evangelion Damhalte*, or gospel harmony, of the second century to the more literal Peshitto version of the fifth century. Coptic developed into a language of worship and scriptural commentary a bit later, in the fourth century, which has traditionally been connected to the work of Shenouda the Archimandrite. Armenian, drawing on Syriac and Greek traditions, created a sacred scripture, liturgy, and commentaries in the fifth century. Of course, just as Greek-speaking Byzantines feared, within each of these languages interpretative traditions developed that the Greek-speaking Christians viewed as heterodox.

Wulfila's fourth-century translation of the Bible into Gothic, which so fascinated nineteenth-century German scholars such as Massmann, should be seen as part of the same translation process. Perhaps even more significant than simply the translation of scripture into Gothic, however, was the appearance in Gothic of Bishop Theodor of Herakleia's commentary on the Gospel of John—the text edited by Massmann under the title *Skeireins* that we discussed in chapter 1. Rather than a monument of Germanic identity, this text should be seen as evidence that, just as was the case with other Eastern languages, Gothic was becoming a language in which not only scripture but also a critical apparatus with which to study scripture might be elaborated.[7]

In the West, language and religion did not become an explicit issue until the late eighth century, and then only in the context of Carolingian linguistic reform and the evangelization of the Germanic- and Slavic-speaking populations in the expanding Frankish empire.

Within the Latin-speaking world, the gradual evolution of spoken Latin was reflected in the way that Latin was written, including in the way that manuscripts of Jerome's Vulgate translation of the Bible were copied. Even in the sixth century Cassiodorus, the distinguished advisor of Ostrogothic kings who retired from the chaos of warfare to his monastic retreat at Vivarium, warned against allowing errors to slip into biblical texts. In his *Institutions of Divine and Secular Learning*, he cautions against hypercorrection—changing accepted usages in biblical texts that may be contrary to established Latin grammar and style. However, he also warned that one should correct corruptions of the text that have resulted from such substitutions as *b* for *v*, *v* for *b*, *o* for *v*, or *n* for *m*, or through adding superfluous aspirates or failing to include appropriate ones. He was concerned about the confusion over which prepositions govern the ablative and the accusative, the proper declination of nouns, and the proper formation of adverbs.[8] Some of these may have been simple errors of ignorance; others undoubtedly reflect changes in the usages of Late Latin, changes that Cassiodorus wished to exclude from the translation of scripture. He echoes Augustine in recommending that if a manuscript of scripture contains words that make no sense, they should be corrected through consulting Jerome's translation, the Greek original, or even, if possible, the original Hebrew or Hebrew teachers. Nevertheless, Cassiodorus considers the received Latin translation of scripture a divine gift: "Let the Holy Spirit hear that most pure form of what it has given, let it receive again unharmed that which it bestowed."[9]

But Cassiodorus's desire to freeze the language of the Latin scriptures appears to have met with only limited success. In the seventh and early eighth centuries, copies of scripture show evidence of the transformations of Late Latin. Surviving biblical and liturgical manuscripts from the eighth century show exactly the kinds of "errors" that indicate the evolving nature of spoken Latin and that appear in other sorts of texts.[10] It might not be too much of an exaggeration to say that as Latin changed, the practices of scribal transmission ensured that the translation of scripture remained closely connected to the spoken idiom. It was only with the educational reforms instituted under Charlemagne that the writing and pronunciation of written Latin abruptly diverged from the spoken idiom. At the same time, both external missionary activity and, equally important, an emphasis on internal conversion undertaken by Anglo-Saxon missionaries in collaboration with the Carolingians led to explicit consideration of the language in which scripture, commentary, and the essentials of the faith ought to be transmitted.

For ideological as well as practical reasons, the reformed Latin of Alcuin was the only formal public language. The wider aspects of this ideological program will be explored in more detail in the next chapter. The effect on biblical translations was immediate: Alcuin's own work on correcting the Vulgate resulted in the systematic removal of those elements of linguistic development that had silently crept into scripture and liturgy. Written and read aloud according to his "reformed" system, the language of scripture was increasingly conceived as something different from the *lingua romana* of ordinary speech.[11]

But was the reformed Latin of the Vulgate a sacred language? Did it have a privileged place in Christian worship? Those who believed it did cited John, 19:19–20, in which Pilate orders that above Christ's cross be written—in Hebrew, Greek, and Latin— "Jesus the Nazarene, King of the Jews." The issue was specifically addressed in 794 at the great reform synod of Frankfurt, which dealt with a variety of weighty issues, including Greek iconoclasm and Spanish adoptionism. The assembly explicitly condemned the belief "that God should only be invoked in three languages, since God is adored in all languages and, if he petitions justly, a person will be heard."[12]

Carolingians were well aware that scripture and even the liturgy had already been translated into a Germanic language by the Goths. Walafrid Strabo, in his treatise on the history of the liturgy, attributes the presence of Greek loan words in Germanic dialects to Goths who had served in the Roman army. He goes on to say that they had translated scripture (*divinos libros*) into their language and even reports that he has learned from a credible monastic brother that among the Scythian peoples, especially the inhabitants of Tomis, the divine office was still celebrated in that language.[13]

The first Carolingian attempt to translate scripture into a Germanic language quite possibly arose in connection with the issues of the synod. Around the same time, someone in the eastern part of the Carolingian Empire, probably in Bavaria, produced a collection of vernacular texts that contained an explicit defense of the use of the vernacular for religious purposes. The first text in the collection, known as the Mondsee Fragments, was discovered among the manuscripts that came to the public library of Linz and the imperial library in Vienna after the dissolution of the monastery of Mondsee in 1791. The first edition of portions of the fragments was published in 1834 by the library's Scriptor Stephan Endlicher and August Heinrich Hoffmann von Fallersleben, a bibliophile, philologist, collector, liberal politician, poet, and composer of the German national hymn.[14] A second edition appeared in 1841, revised by our friend Hans Ferdinand Massmann.

The first of the fragmentary texts was a close, literal translation into Old High German of the Gospel of Matthew, accompanied by the Latin text. This gospel, which ends with the exhortation to "go forth and teach all nations," is immediately followed by a homily on evangelization, *De vocatione gentium*. The homily uses biblical citations to justify the use of the vernacular for divine worship. It explains that after God scattered the peoples following the construction of the tower of Babel, many languages have been used throughout the world, and that, according to Saint Paul, "if then I do not grasp the meaning of what someone is saying, I am a foreigner to the speaker, and he is a foreigner to me" (1 Cor. 14:11). The homilist goes on to cite a wide variety of other scriptural verses, including Psalm 116 ("O praise the Lord, all ye nations: praise him, all ye people"), as part of an extended defense of the vernacular. He makes the argument that it is not a common language that unites Christians, but rather mutual love and a common faith, and he contrasts this with the Jewish people, who were united by a common language but who tried to prevent Paul from preaching to the gentiles. The final portions of the manuscript contained Augustine's sermon on the Gospel of Matthew and excerpts from Isidore of Seville's *On the Catholic Faith against the Jews*, which is not so much an anti-Jewish polemic as it is a summary of Trinitarian beliefs.[15]

All of these texts seem to have as their unifying theme evangelization, whether understood as missions to pagans or as part of an internal mission to Germanic-speaking regions of the Carolingian empire. A very similar, perhaps identical, impulse gave rise to the so-called Freising Fragments discussed in chapter 1. Far from representing the unique linguistic forms of a unique Alp-Slavic or proto-Slovenian language, they actually represent attempts by missionaries to produce evangelization texts in a form of Slavic spoken—with, as has been recently argued, infinite variations—in the Alpine region.[16]

It is often claimed that the impulse represented by the Mondsee Fragments and other early bilingual texts to develop a Christian vernacular was opposed by the Council of Aachen in 817 for all but the most basic instruction. It is difficult to sustain the argument that the Mondsee texts represented an attempt to elevate a Germanic dialect to the status of a fully literate language. After all, the texts are bilingual and serve more as aids to someone with weak Latin than as independent texts. Furthermore, even after the 817 council, other ninth-century authors defended the translation of scripture in similar terms, and not simply for the conversion of pagans. In fact, it was only toward the middle of the century that such texts appeared without their Latin counterparts.

In the Latin preface to *Otfrids Evangelienbuch* (Franconian Gospel Harmony), composed between 862 and 871, Otfrid of Weissenburg made similar claims about the suitability of translating scripture into the language of the faithful. He explained that some of the brethren and a noble lady named Judith had complained that although Juvencus, Arator, and Prudentius had "ornamented the words and miracles of Christ in their own tongue, we, although instructed in the same faith and by that same faith, have been sluggish to translate the great splendor of the divine words into our own language."[17] It was right and proper, Otfrid continued, that "anyone who suffers from the difficulty of understanding a foreign language should know the most sacred words in his own language in order that understanding the law in his own language he would shrink from deviating from it in the slightest way through his own thoughts."[18]

A similar sentiment appears in the preface to the Arabic translation of the psalter composed by Hafs ibn Albar al Quti, or Hafs the Goth, a Mozarab working probably around 880. The prose preface to Hafs's translation explains that the psalter forms the basis of all Christian prayer, and that every people has sung the psalter in its own language:

> The apostle tells us that when the Greeks, Jews, Persians, and Romans first came to believe, they only did so, and only prayed, in the language they knew. The Greeks prayed in Greek, the Syrians in Syriac, the Persians [in Persian and the Latins] in Latin, and this was so that each language affirmed its faith in God. Thus the prayer of Christians, in the East of the land as in the West, that of their bishops, their kings, their patriarchs, of their monks and of the entirety of their popula-

tions, those of the Franks, the Arabs, and the Syrians—all those who
believe in Christ—their entire prayer reposes on the psalter, translated from the Hebrew into many languages such as Greek, Latin,
Syriac, Indian, and Arabic as well as other languages.[19]

For Hafs, just as for Otfrid, it was only natural for every people
to have the scripture in their own language.

Near the end of the ninth century, King Alfred the Great of
Wessex (849–89) voiced a similar attitude toward the importance
of accessing scripture in the vernacular in his famous preface to
his translation of Gregory the Great's *Pastoral Care:* "Then I remembered how the law was first known in Hebrew, and again,
when the Greeks had learnt it, they translated the whole of it
into their own language, and all other books besides. And again
the Romans, when they had learnt it, they translated the whole
of it through learned interpreters into their own language. And
also all other Christian nations translated a part of them into
their own language."[20]

This famous passage resonates with Otfrid's and Hafs's previous arguments, but it already reveals a subtle change from
the two earlier translators' understanding of translation of
scripture. They had spoken of the importance of translating
the "splendor of the divine words." Alfred's argument takes
an unexpected turn. Although he begins with the significance
of the Greeks' and Romans' translations of the divine law into
their own languages, his preface is not, as might be expected
from that sentiment, a preface to a translation, paraphrase, or
harmony of scripture but rather to Gregory's *Pastoral Care.* Alfred adds that other people have also translated "other books"
and goes on to say that it seems appropriate to translate "certain books, which are most needful for all men to know." But is
scripture among these?

Anglo-Saxons made certainly numerous translations of scripture, although it is not entirely clear to what extent Alfred himself was directly responsible for any of these, other than the portions of the Ten Commandments and the Pentateuch incorporated into the preface to his laws. Aside from glosses, the most significant, free-standing translations of scripture into Anglo-Saxon include the Wessex gospels and the Old English Heptateuch, which contains Ælfric's translation of the first part of Genesis.[21]

Ælfric was the most extensive translator of scripture into Old English that we know. He also voiced concerns about translation, concerns that echo patristic anxieties about interpretation and that would develop into even more significant objections to vernacular scripture in the following centuries. As he explained in his preface to his translation of Genesis:

> Now I am concerned lest the work should be dangerous for me or any one else to undertake, because I fear that, if some foolish man should read this book or hear it read, he would imagine that he could live now, under the New Dispensation, just as the patriarchs lived before the old law was established, or as men lived under the law of Moses. At one time I was aware that a certain mass priest, who was then my master, and who had some knowledge of Latin, had in his possession the book of Genesis; he did not scruple to say that the patriarch Jacob had four wives—two sisters and their two handmaids. What he said was true enough, but neither did he realize, nor did I as yet, what a difference there is between the Old Dispensation and the new.[22]

Still, it should be remembered that the distinction for Ælfric was strictly between the learned and the semi-learned: his example of someone who misunderstood the true meaning of scripture was not a layman but a priest, and the version of Genesis that led him astray was not a translation such as the one that Ælfric was undertaking but a text in Latin.

An alternative to literal, and thus potentially misleading, translations was of course paraphrased texts, and both Anglo-Saxon and continental biblical scholars took on the complex task of transmitting biblical material into vernacular culture. The results, whether Old English biblical texts such as Caedmon's Hymn, the Genesis A and B, or the Heliand, do more than translate and explicate. Reworking biblical material to recast it in familiar heroic verse led to the creation of a hybrid form, incorporating elements of two worlds, in which the remembered pagan world remains present even if transformed, and the biblical and Christian content is adjusted to this new existence.[23]

A hint of anxiety concerning translation appears not only in Ælfric but also in Hafs, who defends his program of translation against the inarticulate and stupid who, out of jealousy and viciousness, want to criticize the learned even while benefiting from their efforts.[24]

Nowhere was the use of vernacular scripture more debated during the ninth century than in debates about the use of the Slavic liturgy in the recently converted regions of Moravia and Dalmatia, debates that pitted Frankish churchmen against Rome in their efforts to control the ecclesiastical life in these regions. Although initially opposed to the use of the Slavic language for celebration of the mass, in 880 Pope John VIII granted Methodius permission to perform the mass in Slavic. The pope did so using a subtle intellectual argument in harmony with what was by then a long-established tradition. To summarize his justification:

> We rightly praise Slavonic writing, . . . and order that the praises and the works of Christ our Lord be explained in that same language. For we are instructed by sacred authority that the Lord should not

be praised in only three languages but rather in all languages. Nor is it in any way contrary to sound faith or doctrine either to sing the mass in the Slavonic language or to read the holy gospel, or the divine readings of the New and Old Testament if they have been well translated and interpreted, or to sing all of the other hours of the divine office, because He who made the three principal languages, that is Hebrew, Greek, and Latin, also created all of the others to his praise and glory.[25]

John's argument—that all languages are created by God, and that both scripture and liturgy may be conducted using them—is consonant with antique understandings of scripture and resonates with other ninth-century attitudes toward the use of vernacular and the validity of translating God's word, even to the point of drawing on the same scriptural authorities.

But this was the last defense of the vernacular that the West would see for centuries. John's successor, Stephen V—calling Methodius's liturgy "superstition" and demanding conformity to Roman practice—reversed this permission following the death of Methodius and forbade the use of the Slavic liturgy.[26] In the following century, the Slavic liturgy became widely used in Croatia, although it is difficult to judge reactions to it accurately because our evidence derives from later and dubious sources. For the tenth century, that evidence consists of a condemnation by Pope John X in letters summoning a regional council in 924 or 925, transmitted (if not invented or at least interpolated) by the anonymous sixteenth-century author of the *Historia Salonitana Maior*.[27] The prohibition, however, was based not on the use of the vernacular language itself but rather primarily on the claim that the Croatian church was a particular son of Rome and owed its obedience to Rome: "Because no son should speak or know other than what the father taught him."[28] The issue is not one of language or even of orthodoxy, merely a matter of discipline.

Nevertheless, even if John's letters are genuine, they were apparently largely ignored by the bishops at the council, and it is clear that the Slavic liturgy continued alongside the Latin.

In the middle of the following century, the use of the Slavic liturgy in Croatia again became the object of papal concern. According to the *Historia Salonitana*, written in the thirteenth century by Thomas of Split, a regional synod—convened by the papal legate Maynard on the order of Pope Alexander II in 1061—condemned the use of the Slavic liturgy.[29] This time, apparently, the grounds were not simply conformity to Roman usage but orthodoxy. According to Thomas, heresy was involved: "For they said that a certain heretic called Methodius had devised a Gothic alphabet, and he perniciously wrote a great deal of falsehood against the teachings of the Catholic faith in that same Slavic language."[30]

The condemnation of the Slavic liturgy by the synod convened by Alexander's legate is likely to have been genuine: Maynard—a former monk of the abbey at Monte Cassino and abbot of Pomposa, who had been created a cardinal by Leo IX— was a strong reformer and proponent of papal conformity.[31] It is much less clear whether this condemnation was based on the accusation that Methodius was a heretic. Earlier in his text, Thomas, himself a strong opponent of the Methodian liturgy, confused the Goths with the Slavs in his account of the conquest of Croatia, and his suggestion that Methodius had created a "Gothic" alphabet in which he had written falsehoods is probably an embellishment by Thomas, who confused the Glagolitic script with the Gothic.

Nevertheless, by the reign of Gregory VII, at the height of the radical reform of Western Christianity, papal opposition to the use of the Slavic language in the liturgy was well established. In the winter of 1079–80, Duke Wratislav II of Bohemia petitioned Gregory to allow the use of the Slavic language in the performance of the liturgy. Gregory, who always demanded conformity to what he regarded as the most ancient traditions of the Roman church as embodied by his papal predecessors' decrees, absolutely forbade the practice.[32]

However, although the use of this vernacular liturgy had previously been condemned in the name of Roman discipline, the importance of the sacred languages, and even orthodoxy, Gregory's argument was radical, perhaps even unprecedented. He argued that "from pondering this frequently it is clear that it was pleasing to God the Almighty not without reason that sacred scripture in certain places should be hidden, lest, if it should appear open to all, by chance it might be vulgarized and subjected to disrespect, or that it be so misunderstood by those of little intelligence that it might lead them into error."[33] In other words, God intended certain portions of scripture to be unintelligible to the ignorant, and therefore it is proper that the liturgy, which incorporates the language of scripture, should be performed in a language unintelligible except to the learned.

This argument, although applied specifically to the use of the Slavic liturgy, is actually not about the liturgy at all but rather about the scriptural elements contained therein, and thus ultimately about the accessibility of scripture to the laity. This argument is a direct challenge to the tradition that we have seen develop since late antiquity: that precisely because of the obscurity of scripture, it was necessary to give the laity access to it within a context of proper interpretation. For previous (and many subsequent) authorities, the solution to the obscurity of scripture was proper preaching, explication, and commentaries—which, far from maintaining the obscurity of scripture, sought rather to bring these secrets to the whole world.

The argument that worship should be conducted only in a sacred language had been condemned since at least the synod of Frankfurt and had been explicitly rejected by John VIII. The issue of conformity to Roman practice was much more in the forefront of Gregory's thoughts and deeds. His condemnation of the use of vernacular should be seen rather in the context of his equally firm condemnation of the use of other liturgies in the West, including the Ambrosian and especially the Mozarabic. Neither of these were performed in the vernacular, yet Gregory—faithful to his attempt to enforce Roman practice as widely as possible—rejected both, as well as innovations in Roman liturgy introduced by Frankish and later German kings and popes in the two centuries preceding his own election. In the case of the Mozarabic liturgy, he was particularly adamant, finding this ritual suspect because of the Priscillianist and Arian traditions of Spain. He condemned it, as E. J. C. Cowdery suggests, as "no better than a superstitious deceit."[34] As with the apparent condemnation of the Slavic liturgy by John X, for Gregory the fundamental issue was his belief that from ancient times the church of Spain had belonged "to Saint Peter and the holy Roman Church in *ius et proprietatem*."[35]

Language, then, appears to be a secondary issue in the context of eleventh-century liturgical concerns. Nevertheless, Gregory's novel argument about the importance of deliberate obfuscation of the mysteries of scripture might be seen as the culmination of a growing concern in various regions of Europe across the tenth century. From the confident value of scriptural translation expressed by Otfrid to the defensive stance of Hafs and the anxieties of Ælfric, one sees an increasing malaise at the thought of the words of scripture actually reaching the ignorant. Such anxieties were obviously not new—they are at least as ancient as Augustine and Jerome—but the solution was radical. Augustine, in his great treatise *On Christian Doctrine*, had argued that the obscurities of scripture should be dealt with through proper education and careful preaching and explication to the faithful, not by hiding the content from them in a foreign language. The concern is not really about heresy, as it will be in the twelfth century—when, particularly in the south of France, vernacular translations of scripture will be increasingly identified with heterodox lay movements—but rather of distinguishing between those with the wisdom and understanding to penetrate the mysteries of scripture as it is communicated in liturgy and those who, primarily the laity or unreformed clergy (be they Anglo-Saxon mass priests or Croatian clerics), cannot be trusted with the word of God. Essentially the issue, as it was for those who attacked Jerome for his knowledge and use of Syriac, was one of control: the power of the reformed church demanded exclusive authority over the word of God, and this authority meant that the word of God and his worship could take place only in an idiom emanating from the Roman center. But by claiming Latin to be the exclusive language of the liturgy, and by claiming that the use of Latin explicitly and intentionally excluded a portion of the Christian faithful from understanding the words of scripture, Latin was thereby claimed as the language of the church and not the common language of all powers, secular as well as religious.

Gregory's assertion that the mysteries of scripture should be kept hidden from the faithful seems not to have been repeated— this baldfaced assertion of clerical privilege was too much even for his successors. However, the effect of claiming Latin as the medium of sacred knowledge marked an important turning point in the linguistic ideology of Europe. Explicitly a language designed to hide rather than to communicate, Latin was on its way to the position that King Rudolf of Habsburg felt it should hold. He demanded in the thirteenth century that people in his court should use not Latin but German "because," he is said to have declared, "the difficulties of Latin were producing errors, grave doubts and deceiving laymen." [36] We will return to secular power and language in our final chapter.

# 3 Vernacular Language and Secular Power in Emerging Europe

The last chapter traced the failure of Western vernaculars to become vehicles for Christian worship between the end of antiquity and the eleventh century. In this chapter we will examine the gradual appearance of the written vernacular in the exercise of secular power in the early Middle Ages, a period during which, except in Anglo-Saxon England, the vernacular was never the normal vehicle for textualizing public authority. Nowhere did the sporadic use of vernacular during this long period constitute the beginnings of a gradual and inevitable rise of the vernacular. Indeed, a recent and important colloquium on the relationship between Latin and vernacular languages carried the title "the resistible ascension of vernaculars."[1]

The process was neither linear nor inevitable. Only very gradually, from the tenth century to the fifteenth, did vernacular languages become normal written media for the use of chancelleries, law courts, and aristocratic institutions. In royal chancelleries, Serge Lusignan has shown that the process was not completed in Castille until the thirteenth century; in France, not until the fourteenth; and in England, only in the fifteenth. In parts of Eastern Europe, the process would not be complete until the nineteenth.[2] Nor could this process take place without a transformation of the vernaculars themselves. Lusignan has argued that before French or English could replace Latin as the normal written language of the French and English monarchies, these vernaculars had to undergo serious latinization. Thomas Brunner, who has traced the gradual introduction of the vernacular into archival practice across Western Europe, has found much the same thing as Lusignan: with the clear exception of Anglo-Saxon England (and the possible exception of Ireland and Wales), vernaculars only gradually became normal languages of record keeping between the eleventh and fifteenth centuries.[3] Brunner recognizes that one must be careful to avoid overgeneralizations about this phenomenon, bearing in mind that very specific circumstances determined how and when the vernacular was adopted in each society. In some areas—particularly certain regions where Romance languages such as Occitan, Catalan, and Castilian were spoken—the process took place gradually, beginning as early as the tenth or eleventh century with the appearance of what has been termed *latin farci*, texts in Latin containing isolated words or even phrases, usually toponyms but also technical terms, in the vernacular.[4] Elsewhere—not only in Germanic, Celtic, and Slavic regions but also in places such as France—the vernacular appeared later but abruptly alongside or in place of Latin, without an intermediate phase of bilingual or mixed texts.

If the "how" of this transformation differed across Europe, so too did the "why." Whatever the causes of such transformations, older hypotheses such as the speculation that scribes were forced to turn to the vernacular because of their declining ability to write in Latin or the development of vernaculars as expressions of national identity must be rejected. In many areas of Europe, scribes who prepared documents in the vernacular continued to prepare others in Latin: the choice of language was strategic, not a linguistic necessity. Furthermore, the vernacular did not necessarily represent the use of the ordinary speech of the local community. Certain prestige vernaculars such as French replaced written Latin in areas where it remained the spoken vernacular, and elsewhere standardized or even artificial dialects that were not in ordinary usage were chosen for use in documents.

Part of this strategic move from Latin to other languages relates directly to the development we have examined in the previous chapter. After the linguistic reforms of the late eighth century, Latin was, in the Frankish empire and its successor kingdoms, essentially and ideologically the language of government, law, and administration. It was the language of religion, too, but not exclusively so. Progressively, however, as we have seen, ecclesiastical consolidation created an ideological role for Latin closely related to the mysteries of the Christian faith and the domain of the clergy. The movement away from Latin as the language of secular power should be understood at least in part as a result of the increasing identification of Latin as the language of the clergy. The most explicit example of this is the substitution of German for Latin in the German empire, a process that began fairly abruptly, as Brunner has shown, first with a charter of Counts Albert and Rudolf of Habsburg issued in 1238 and then a diploma of King Conrad IV in 1240.[5] What this may have meant can best be understood by considering Rudolf's attitude toward Latin following his election as King of the Romans in 1273. In 1275 at the Reichstag in Augsburg, Bishop Bernard of Seckau—the representative of Rudolf's rival, the Bohemian King Ottokar II—attempted to raise objections to Rudolf's election in a long and elegant Latin address. Rudolf interrupted him, insisting that to avoid deception the matter should be discussed in German rather than Latin.[6] According to the chronicler John of Viktring, Rudolf also demanded that his chancellery use German rather than Latin because, as we saw at the end of the last chapter, he contended that Latin was producing errors and deceiving laymen.[7] Such sentiments in the German empire coincided with a linguistic usage noted by Rudolf-Dieter Heim in his study of the treatment of Germanic and Romance languages and peoples in Old French poetry, in which "parler en roman sans latin" meant to speak openly.[8] By the thirteenth century, Latin was ideologically positioned as a language of the church—complicated, hidden, and susceptible to manipulation and deception. It was not abandoned by the courts, which continued to use Latin for certain types of documents and in certain correspondence. However, the choice of language could carry an ideological or propagandistic message quite apart from the content of the document itself.

But what about the use of vernaculars in the early Middle Ages? Prior to the twelfth century, except in England, no vernacular language competed with Latin as the primary language of secular authority, nor was there any attempt to introduce such a practice. Still, from late antiquity—when Latin was the undisputed language of command and coercion—through the Carolingian period, the vernacular began to play new and significant roles in the exercise of public authority, roles that suggest new relationships between ruler and ruled that required new strategies of linguistic deployment.

In the tradition of national and nationalist philology that I introduced in chapter 1, there remains a tendency within certain philological and historical traditions—particularly, but not exclusively, the German—to see the deployment of the vernacular as early as the eighth century as part of an ethnic, protonational program. In particular, generations of philologists and historians have attempted to credit Charlemagne, the Frankish ruler who united much of Western Europe at the end of the eighth century, with a linguistic program that valorized the Frankish language. But as I have attempted to suggest, there are other, more fruitful ways of understanding linguistic strategies in the early Middle Ages. Certainly Charlemagne and his successors introduced changes in how language was employed, but these changes hardly amount to a Germanic language policy.

In tracing these changes, I want to emphasize from the outset that my focus is not the development of vernacular languages in general or in particular. Nor am I interested in the often-asked question, "When did Latin cease to be spoken in the Latin West?" My question is rather different: under what conditions did the use of different registers of language—*lingua vulgata, lingua rustica, lingua Theodisca,* and so forth—become an explicit part of the exercise of authority? Under what sociolinguistic conditions did the use of different languages, or of different registers within the same broad language, become sufficiently significant to leave a record?

I assume that people normally communicated in a variety of languages or dialects, but for centuries the language used for this communication was not mentioned, and the language in which communication was described was always Latin or Greek. When not only the content of communication but the language of communication becomes a subject of note, we need to understand why this is the case.

Any such examination must begin with the status of language within the Roman Empire. Of the vast spectrum of languages spoken within the empire other than Latin and Greek, we know surprisingly little. The Gallic languages of the West survive in rare inscriptions, even though as late as around 180 Bishop Irenaeus of Lyons described himself as living among the Keltæ and being accustomed for the most part to use a barbarous dialect.[9] In spite of contemporary Albanian claims of identity with the ancient Illyrians, little remains of ancient Illyrian but names. In the East, of course, Arabic, Punic, and Berber inscriptions—as well as more abundant texts in Syriac, Hebrew, and above all demotic Egyptian and Coptic—have survived to give a much greater understanding of the languages of the eastern Roman Empire. However, knowledge of these languages was not transmitted by Romans themselves. Like other imperialists (I would mention, among others, British, Russians, and of course Americans), the Romans were not only largely ignorant of foreign languages (except for Greek in the Roman case), but they were even proud of their ignorance. Although communication with natives throughout the empire was a necessity, the ability to speak other languages was nothing to brag about, and if we can believe Cicero, some Romans even went so far as to intentionally make errors when speaking Greek, lest they be seen as too comfortable with this foreign idiom. However communication actually occurred, it was represented and recorded as taking place in Latin, the language of the empire.

The replacement of Roman civil and military authority by federated barbarian armies did not initially change this tradition. After all, these Barbari had been part of the Roman military system for generations and were self-consciously assuming roles within the Roman constitutional structure, which indeed was the only structure that they or anyone else could imagine. Like arrivistes in many other cultures, these new aristocrats were eager to adopt the values and marks of the culture they were supplanting. The fifth-century poet and courtier Sidonius Apollinaris (ca. 430–489), for example, praises Arbogast, a descendant of Frankish commanders governing Trier, for his skill in the Latin language, praise the count no doubt enjoyed.[10] Flattering him for a letter dictated by Arbogast that he has received, Sidonius remarks: "You have your conversation among barbarians, yet you permit no barbarism to pass your lips; in eloquence and valor you equal those ancient generals whose hands could wield the stylus no less skillfully than the sword. The Roman tongue is long banished from Belgium and the Rhine; but if its splendor has anywhere survived, it is surely with you; our jurisdiction is fallen into decay along the frontier, but while you live and preserve your eloquence, the Latin language stands unshaken."[11]

And yet Sidonius's praise for this Roman Frank's *latinitas* must be contrasted with the sentiments in another of his letters, this one addressed to his friend Syagrius, a member of a distinguished Roman family. After praising Syagrius as the descendant of one who was not only consul but also a poet, and recalling Syagrius's excellent education, Sidonius describes his friend's mastery of the Germanic language: "You can hardly conceive how amused we all are to hear that, when you are by, not a barbarian but fears to perpetrate a barbarism in his own language. Old Germans bowed with age are said to stand astounded when they see you interpreting their German letters."[12]

Sidonius is clearly teasing his friend, and yet in his closing advice that Syagrius not neglect his reading so that he will not lose his command of Latin, one glimpses some anxiety. The idea that a descendant of Frankish mercenaries such as Arbogast would advance his position through the cultivation of Latin letters fit fully into the venerable tradition of Rome and its openness to those who would acquire a classical education.[13] But to think that the descendant of a Roman consul and poet could advance his position through his command of a barbarous tongue was something new. Nor was Syagrius the only Roman who saw knowledge of a barbarian language as a path to power and preferment. The Ostrogothic king Theodoric praised his *Comes sacrarum largitionum*, Cyprianus, for his ability in three languages: Latin, Greek, and Gothic.[14] Cyprianus also made sure that his sons would acquire an education in Gothic.[15] It is no small irony that the letters in which Cyprianus is praised for this novel education in a barbarian tongue were penned on behalf of Theodoric by Cassiodorus—a man who, like Syagrius, who had risen to the center of power through his command of classical languages and rhetoric, but who was not skilled in the language of his masters or, if he was, never boasted of it.

However, whatever advantages bilingualism might have given to those Romans in the service of barbarian rulers, these languages never found their way into the formal textualization of governance. Burgundians may have admired Syagrius's ability to speak their language, but his Latin eloquence was surely what they turned to as the language of record, and barbarian rulers aspired to the Latinity of an Arbogast for themselves and their children. Cyprianus may have spoken Gothic, but Theodoric employed Cassiodorus, the master of Latin rhetoric, as his secretary.

The only worlds in which a barbarian language was regularly textualized in the conduct of power were those areas that, like Ireland, had never been part of the Roman cultural and linguistic sphere or that, like those Anglo-Saxon kingdoms whose populations had ceased to speak Latin altogether, had no tension between Latin and the vernacular: Latin was not the language of everyday speech and was thus free to take on the most extravagant rhetorical, syntactical, and lexical efflorescence, while the work of preaching, pastoral care, and the common business of life could be conducted in the vernacular without apology or tension with Latinity. In the British Isles, just as later in Scandinavia, the use of the vernacular not only for oral communication but for writing began early and rapidly reached into all spheres of life that involved not only a Latinate clergy but laity from all levels of society.[16]

The situation in the Frankish kingdom, including as it did both Germanic and Romance speakers, was quite different. In Romance-speaking areas, the spoken language and the written language remained closely united well into the eighth century. In Germanic areas, however, Latin remained the language of record while written Germanic was confined to glosses, vocabulary lists, and other tools intended to teach the basics of Latin literacy. The reforms of the Carolingians radically changed the situation. As Regina Maria Dröll and others have argued, the alliance between the Carolingian dynasty and the Roman papacy, and the determination to see the Frankish kingdom as the ideological successor of the Roman Empire, led to a revalorization of Latin culture and, through the agency of Anglo-Saxon missionaries and especially educators such as Alcuin of York, to the creation of new techniques of writing and speaking Latin.[17] The results were by no means an attempt to elevate any of the many vernaculars spoken in the empire into a national language. Rather, as the scholarship of Michel Banniard and Roger Wright has shown us, Carolingian linguistic reform generated an awareness that such reforms were creating linguistic differences between the performance of the commonly spoken Latins within the Romance speaking population and the new imperial Latin language, in which the Carolingian elite, both clerical and lay, was being trained.[18] Indeed the linguistic politics of the Carolingians aimed at the creation not of a politicized vernacular, but rather of what Mayke de Jong has termed a "Mandarin language," which in this case was the reformed Latin of the imperial elite.[19] Mastery of that language, for native speakers of both Latin and Germanic languages, was essential for full participation in the Carolingian program of royal administration and the Christian cult. Like other Mandarin languages, Carolingian Latin not only had a functional value but also was a means of identifying this elite and separating its members from the masses. However, communication with the masses continued to be an essential priority for the elite, especially in the area of religious education and correction, and this meant that for the first time conscious efforts had to be made to bridge the gap between the linguistic register that the elites used self-consciously to mark their status and those used by ordinary men and women. Thus within a generation of these linguistic reforms, one begins to read for the first time about the necessity to preach to the people in an idiom that they could understand. Not surprisingly it was at a council held in 813 in Tours—the city in which Alcuin, as abbot of St. Martin, had most vigorously advanced his linguistic reform program—that the assembled prelates required that homilies be translated into *rustica Romana lingua* and *Theodisca lingua* so that the congregation could more easily understand what was being said.[20]

However, the deep attachment of the earliest Carolingians to a revival of *romanitas* militated against the development of the vernacular, especially Germanic, as part of central policy. Although some scholars have argued that Charlemagne pursued a linguistic policy that sought to advance German as a political tool, such a policy would have run counter to the fundamental unifying program of Carolingian cultural, religious, and political reform. As we noted in the previous chapter, Carolingian churchmen certainly looked to translations of scripture and basic catechetical texts as necessary elements of external and internal conversion. Old High German glosses begin to appear in great numbers—over a thousand extant manuscripts carry some glosses—and bilingual texts, such as translations of Isidore's *De Fide Christiana* and the Mondsee Fragments of biblical and patristic texts, were produced in the late eighth and early ninth centuries. All of these, however, were in various ways either pastoral and missionary or directed toward providing access to Latin authors, both classical and patristic. Even elaborate texts such as the translations of Isidore and the Mondsee texts were expressly bilingual. Rather like the modern Loeb Classics, they were intended not to create a new, independent literary language but to aid those who had a basic, but inadequate, knowledge of Latin.

But if the reign of Charlemagne did not initiate a vernacular renaissance, its linguistic and educational reforms did create a new linguistic consciousness. As we have seen, for the first time conciliar and capitulary directives begin to express explicit concerns about communication in both *rustica Romana lingua* and *Theodisca lingua*. Language became, perhaps for the first time since the fifth century, capable of being instrumentalized and mobilized as a tool of secular authority. In the metaphor of the philologist Franz Bäuml, language could become a character in the staged performance of power.[21] Concretely, this means that not only the content of a speech act carried meaning but that the language or language register in which the act was performed or written could itself have a function, reinforcing the content and conveying a message to the particular audience for which it was intended.

We see the same phenomenon in secular bilingual texts that use code switching as part of their strategy. By inserting or at least invoking another language or language register, not only the content of what is reported but the fact that it is in another language becomes a strategy of representation. Such a process appears from the late eighth century, especially in three boundary descriptions—one of a donation to the monastery of Fulda in 777 and two versions of a boundary description from Würzburg.[22] These documents have been extensively studied by Germanic philologists, in terms both of their language and of the evidence that they present about the introduction of written documentation into traditionally oral forms of property transfer.[23] But what is particularly significant from our perspective is the way in which they are specifically records of public rituals, of performances in which the language itself becomes, as Bäuml suggested, an actor. In each case a group of notables, in the company of royal officials, swore to the boundaries of the donations, the boundaries themselves being described in Old High German. In the first, we are told that twenty-one notables swore to the boundaries;[24] the Würzburg documents include the names of twenty-seven men who made the circumnavigation of the property and then swore to its accuracy.[25] The code switching in these documents is anything but arbitrary: what appears in German is the precise route taken around the boundaries of these estates. In this, the texts closely resemble Anglo-Saxon vernacular boundary descriptions appended to or inserted into Latin charters, following a well-established tradition.[26] The German vernacular texts record both the physical displacements of the royal official and the local witnesses who made the circumnavigations and, most important, the precise descriptions to which they swore. Their oaths, and the readiness of the witnesses to acknowledge having sworn, rather than the documents themselves, was what made the acts of donation valid.[27] One might postulate that, as in the English examples, following the perambulation and the oath, a separate text was prepared in the vernacular that recorded the exact words sworn.[28] Later it was incorporated into the Latin charter.

Prior to the late eighth century—except in Bavaria, where older, late Roman legal traditions were preserved—no Latin charter would have been created in the eastern portions of the Frankish world. Now, ecclesiastical institutions were increasingly turning to texts to preserve their rights. The dramatic events of the perambulation and the public oath sworn by the participating notables were given even greater emphasis by recording them not in a Latin translation but in the vernacular. The notables' sworn statement had to be heard and recorded first in the presence of witnesses and then, secondarily, in a document that could be used as an aide-mémoire of the events. Such documents give particularly important evidence about the relationship between ritual action, oral performance, and memory. One also sees with particular clarity the importance of accessibility of the words spoken and remembered by those participating in the circumnavigation, an importance that favored the use of the vernacular in place names and, at times, just as in England, in the entire description of boundaries. The bilingual text becomes, then, a record not only of a transfer but also of the events and the sounds that accompanied that transfer, sounds that can be reproduced and acknowledged as correct without the intervention of a translator by those who made them or by their descendants. The acknowledgment of the reality of the vernacular thus enabled its explicit incorporation into the performance and written memory of law.

The vernacular, enlisted as an actor in the public performance of power, became even more significant in the aftermath of the disintegration of the Carolingian empire, on the death of Louis the Pious. The often-studied oaths of Strasbourg and the less well known oaths of Koblenz demonstrate even more dramatically the possibilities of co-opting vernacular speech as an instrument of power, even while maintaining the status of reformed Latin as the language of royal administration.

Again, one must not interpret the employment of the vernacular as part of an attempt to create a national language, either in the western kingdom of Charles the Bald or in the eastern region ruled by Louis the German, his half-brother. Rather, the mixture of languages and language registers used language to heighten the performative aspects of rule at a moment when royal authority in both east and west was in jeopardy.

The long-discussed oaths of Strasbourg present graphically the way in which language difference and language unity could be performed.[29] In 842—following the catastrophic battle of Fontenay, at which the armies of Louis the German and Charles the Bald defeated that of Lothar, their brother—Louis and Charles came together to pledge mutual faith and support, a promise that probably neither intended to keep. Nor were their supporters ignorant of their latent hostility: convincing them that the two really meant to be faithful to each other was a major purpose of the public performance of mutual oath taking. The result, as reported by the historian and political actor Nithard, was a carefully choreographed performance in which language was a central actor.

Because Nithard provided the texts of the oaths in *Teudisca lingua* as well as in *Romana lingua*, his text has for centuries been seen on both sides of the Rhine as a fundamental document in the history not only of German and French, but also of Germany and France. Since the sixteenth-century jurist and political philosopher Jean Bodin, the oaths have been seen as significant in the history of the French language. However, the manuscript was sold to Queen Christina of Sweden in the seventeenth century. It was part of the great library she took with her to Rome when she scandalously converted to Catholicism, and thus the document entered the Vatican library along with the rest of her texts after her death. The text was singled out by Napoleon's advisors as one of the manuscripts to be taken to Paris following the conquest of Italy and, following Napoleon's defeat, was found to be "missing" when representatives from the Vatican arrived in Paris to reclaim the French war booty. At the time, it was apparently in the hands of Joseph-Jean-Théophile de Mourcin (1784–1856), a young classicist and archaeologist fascinated with collecting antiquities, who published the text with a commentary in 1815. By then, the Vatican representatives had returned home with a Renaissance Plato manuscript in place of the missing Nithard document. Only in 1869 did Julius Brakelmann, a young German medievalist working in the Bibliothèque Royale, locate the manuscript, with the assistance of unnamed French colleagues who obviously knew of its existence all along. Brakelmann wrote an article reporting his find, but he died in the Franco-Prussian War the next year—a victim, one might say, of the conflict that had begun with the circumstances that led to the oaths of Strasbourg in the ninth century and that had endured for almost a millennium.[30]

Long seen as the mark of division between the Romance and Germanic parts of the Carolingian empire, the text is nothing of the kind. It is, rather, as Rosamond McKitterick and Janet Nelson have argued, a performance of the enduring unity of the empire.[31] First, it is the reformed Latin that is the language of the Carolingian elite, regardless of their ethnic or geographical origins. This is the language employed by Nithard himself, a grandson of Charlemagne, supporter of Charles the Bald, and historian warrior who would die in battle a few years later. Whatever languages and dialects may have been spoken by the kings and their close advisors at Strasbourg, this reformed Latin remains the way that it is textualized, a sign of the still strong cultural bonds uniting the imperial aristocracy.

But the brothers faced the reality that their armies—free warriors drawn from the local gentry who did not belong to the wider, international world represented by the reformed Latin of the elite—no longer trusted their word. As Nithard has Charles say, "since we believe that you doubt our stable firm and fraternal fidelity,"[32] the brothers undertake oaths in registers directly accessible to their followers, but they do so in a way that emphasizes the unity rather than the diversity of their men. First, Louis speaks in *Teudisca lingua* and Charles speaks in *Romana lingua*. But then Louis swears his oath in the language of his brother's army, *Romana lingua*, and then Charles repeats the oath in *Teudisca lingua*. Both brothers were surely trilingual, and both were capable of taking oaths in both vernaculars. The oaths themselves were certainly not ad hoc, as some have suggested, and must have been carefully worked out in advance. The language is technical and suggests that the entire performance was, as

Gerd Althoff has suggested for other medieval rituals of power, carefully prepared ahead of time.[33] By each swearing in both languages, the brothers emphasize that they continue to represent a united *regnum Francorum*.

A similar performance of language register took place some sixteen years later at Koblenz, where—after an unsuccessful invasion of Charles's kingdom by Louis—the two brothers met once more to try to settle their differences.[34] Again, the actual reconciliation took place in private, in the church of St. Castor, and the report of this event, witnessed by bishops and counts in both kings' entourages—that is, by the elite—is entirely in Latin and makes no use of the vernacular.[35]

However, following the reconciliation, the status of those of Charles's vassals who had joined his brother's expedition against him needed to be clarified. Again, at this level of society, language became a performer in the public drama of reconciliation.

First, Louis announced their agreement in *lingua Theodisca*. Then Charles recapitulated the same agreement in *Romana lingua* before summarizing it in *lingua Theodisca*. Following this, Louis asked Charles in *lingua Romana* what he intended to do about those of his men who had supported Louis. Charles— speaking, as the text says, in a very loud voice (*excelsiori voce*)— in *lingua Romana* outlined the conditions according to which the rebels could keep their benefices they had received from Charles's predecessors. Then Louis, in *lingua Theodisca*, consented to the agreement, and Charles closed the proceedings in *lingua Romana*.

Again, as at Strasbourg, the brothers, probably reading from carefully prepared written scripts, performed for their armies in both languages. Each addressed the other's followers in their vernacular. However, the performance was what mattered: as in the boundary oaths, here were the words, direct and without need of translation, performed before those for whom they were most significant, in a way that brought them directly into the exercise of royal power.

There is no need to posit primitive Germanic ideas about the magic of oaths to justify either of these performances, especially considering the fact that the vernacular was deemed just as appropriate for the Romance-speaking armies as it was for the Germanic-speaking ones. Nor need we assume that these oaths represented a self-conscious political program of cultivation of either dialect within the brothers' kingdoms.

Certainly, by the middle of the ninth century, as we saw in the previous chapter, texts intended for devotional purposes were beginning to appear in German dialects, most significantly Otfrid of Weissenburg's Gospel harmony.[36] Otfrid belonged to a network of monks and courtiers bringing the learning of the great Alemannic monasteries of St. Gall, Reichenau, and Weissenburg to the court of Louis the German, and his dedication of this work to Louis clearly emphasizes the latter's legitimacy as God's representative and the status of his Frankish people as *thiot gotes* (the people of God).

None of this, however, meant that the East Frankish kingdom was attempting to elevate Frankish, or any other Germanic dialect, to the level of a national language, any more than the *lingua Romana* texts of Charles or other devotional and religious materials in Romance vernaculars meant that the West Frankish kingdom was attempting to use proto-French to strengthen national identity, or the presence of very similar Slavic texts in the Freising Fragments implied a Slovenian or Slavic national identity. Language had become a potential instrument in the performance of secular power, to be mobilized especially in circumstances when justice or royal affairs needed to be performed before a wide, popular audience. But this strategy—with apologies to the generations of French, German, Slavic, and other philologists who sought such a strategy in the fragments of ancient vernacular documents—did not constitute an ideology, still less a national language ideology. If such strategy existed, it proved ephemeral: as the Carolingian realm fragmented into truly separate kingdoms, even these occasional employments of the vernacular in the recording of acts of power became less rather than more frequent. Neither in the western kingdom of Charles the Bald nor in the eastern kingdom of Louis the German was any further effort made to record, or even to note, vernacular language use: language simply did not appear among the various strategies used for the mobilization of unity. For that one would have to wait centuries, or perhaps to look to Anglo-Saxon England. But that is another story for another time.

# Notes

FOREWORD

*Opening address to Professor Patrick J. Geary's Jerusalem Lecture in History in Memory of Menahem Stern, 4 May 2010.*

INTRODUCTION

1  A good introduction to social linguistics is Linda Thomas and Shân Wareing, eds., *Language, Society and Power: An Introduction* (London: Routledge, 1999). On the use of language not simply to communicate but to divide, placed in the context of early medieval Europe, see Wolfgang Haubrichs, "Differenz und Identität—Sprache als Instrument der Kommunikation und der Gruppenbildung im frühen Mittelalter," in *Sprache und Identität im frühen Mittelalter,* , ed. Walter Pohl and Bernhard Zeller (Vienna: Verlag der Österreichen Akademie der Wissenschaften, 2012), 23–38.

2  Jacqueline Urla, "Ethnic Protest and Social Planning: A Look at Basque Language Revival," *Cultural Anthropology* 3, no. 4 (1988): 379–94.

3  "Nec non et illud sciendum, quod, sicut diversae nationes populorum inter se discrepant genere moribus lingua legibus,

ita sancta universalis aecclesia toto orbe terrarum diffusa, quamvis in unitate fidei coniungatur, tamen consuetudinibus aecclesiasticis ab invicem differt" ("Reginonis abbatis Prumiensis Chronicon cum continuatione Treverensi," *Epistula Reginonis ad Hathonem Archiepiscopum Missa, Prefatio Operis Subsequentis*, xix–xx, in *MGH Scriptores rerum Germanicarum in usum scholarum separatim editi* 50, ed. Friedrich Kurze [Hanover: Hahn, 1890]). On Regino's criteria, see Wolfgang Haubrichs, "Ethnizität zwischen Differenz und Identität. Sprache als Instrument der Kommunikation und der Gruppenbildung im frühen Mittelalter," *Zeitschrift für Literaturwissenschaft und Linguistik* 164 (2011): 10–38, especially 33–35.

4  On the complex prehistory of national identity in the examples of Germany and Italy, see Caspar Hirschi, *Wettkampf der Nationen: Konstruktionen einer deutschen Ehrgemeinschaft an der Wende vom Mittelalter zur Neuzeit* (Göttingen: Wallstein, 2005).

5  "Tout confirme donc que chaque langue exprime le caractère du peuple qui la parle" (Étienne Bonnot de Condillac, "Essai sur l'origine des connaissances humaines," in *Œuvres philosophiques de Condillac*, ed. Georges Le Roy, vol. 1 [Paris: Presses universitaires de France, 1947], part II, section I, chapter 15, no. 143, 98).

6  Ibid., 98–99.

7  "En effet, qu'on remonte de siècles en siècles, on verra que plus notre langue a été barbare, plus nous avons été éloignés de connoître la langue latine, et nous n'avons commencé à écrire bien en latin, que quand nous avons été capables de le faire en français" (ibid., 100).

8  "Il faut remarquer que dans une langue qui ne s'est pas formée des débris de plusieurs autres, les progrès doivent être beaucoup plus prompts, parce qu'elle a dès son origine un caractère: c'est pourquoi les Grecs ont eu de bonne heure d'excellents écrivains" (ibid).

9  Hans Aarsleff, "The Tradition of Condillac: The Problem of the Origin of Language in the Eighteenth Century and the Debate

in the Berlin Academy before Herder," in Hans Aarsleff, *From Locke to Saussure, Essays on the Study of Language and Intellectual History* (Minneapolis: University of Minnesota Press, 1982), 146–209.

10 For an intelligent overview of language in the exercise of power during the early Middle Ages that complements the approach I follow in this book, see Julia M. H. Smith, *Europe after Rome: A New Cultural History 500–1000* (Oxford: Oxford University Press, 2005), chap. 1, "Rome Speaking and Writing."

## I. INVENTING THE LINGUISTIC MONUMENTS OF EUROPE

*This chapter has greatly benefited from the advice of colleagues in the focus group Medievalism, Archaic Origins and Regimes of Historicity: Alternatives to Antique Tradition in the Nineteenth Century in East-Central, Southeast and Northern Europe, as well as from Sarah Kay and the participants in Princeton University's Shelby Cullom Davis Center, where I presented a preliminary version.*

1 Johann Gottlieb Fichte, *Reden an die deutsche Nation*, ed. Alexander Aichele (Hamburg: Felix Meiner Verlag, 2008), 60–76.

2 Joep Leerssen, "Introduction: Philology and the European Construction of National Literatures," in *Editing the Nation's Memory: Textual Scholarship and Nation-Building in 19th-Century Europe*, eds. Dirk Van Hulle and Joep Leerssen (Amsterdam: Rodopi, 2008), 13–27; Joep Leerssen, "Literary Historicism: Romanticism, Philologists, and the Presence of the Past," *Modern Language Quarterly* 65, no. 2 (2004): 221–43.

3 See, in particular, Leerssen, "Introduction."

4 Thus, along with representatives of the Vatican Library, Jacob Grimm was sent to Paris to recover books from Hesse-Kassel, while Jernej Kopitar was in Paris on a similar mission from Vienna. Hans Ferdinand Massmann was in Paris as a member of a volunteer military unit at the same time that Grimm was

there, and the two were thus able to meet. On the recovery of manuscripts confiscated by Napoleon, see Anthony Hobson, "Appropriations from Foreign Libraries during the French Revolution and Empire," *Bulletin du bibliophile*, no. 2 (1989): 255–72; Marie Pierre Laffitte, "La Bibliothèque nationale et les 'conquêtes artistiques' de la Révolution et de l'Empire: les manuscrits d'Italie (1796–1815)," *Bulletin du bibliophile*, no. 2 (1989): 273–323. For earlier reflections on the process from the German perspective, see Ernst Steinmann, "Die Plünderung Roms durch Bonaparte," *Internationale Monatsschrift für Wissenschaft Kunst und Technik* 11, no. 6 (1917): cols. 641–76, 819–75. For a French defense of Napoleon's confiscations, see Eugène Muntz, "Les invasions de 1814–1815 et la spoliation de nos musées (Episodes d'histoire diplomatique)," *La Nouvelle Revue*, April 1897, 703–16; July 1897, 193–207; August 1897, 420–39. I am grateful to Courtney Booker for bringing these studies to my attention.

5   On Mai, see Antonio Carrannante, "Angelo Mai," in *Dizionario biografico degli Italiani* (Rome: Istituto della Enciclopedia italiana, 2006), 67:517–520.

6   Tom Shippey, "The Case of Beowulf," in *Editing the Nation's Memory: Textual Scholarship and Nation-Building in 19th-Century Europe*, ed. Dirk Van Hulle and Joep Leerssen (Amsterdam: Rodopi, 2008), 223–39; Tom Shippey and Andreas Haarder, eds., *Beowulf: The Critical Heritage* (London: Routledge, 1988); Magnús Fjalldal, "To Fall by Ambition: Grímur Thorkelín and His Beowulf Edition," *Neophilologus* 92, no. 2 (2008): 321–32.

7   See, most recently, Ingrid Merchiers, *Cultural Nationalism in the South Slav Habsburg Lands in the Early Nineteenth Century: The Scholarly Network of Jernej Kopitar (1780–1844)* (Munich: Verlag Otto Sagner, 2007); Darko Dolinar, "Slovene Text Editions, Slavic Philology and Nation-Building," in *Editing the Nation's Memory: Textual Scholarship and Nation-Building in 19th-Century Europe*, ed. Dirk Van Hulle and Joep Leerssen, (Amsterdam: Rodopi, 2008), 65–78.

8  On Graff, see Wilhelm Scherer, "Graff, Eberhard Gottlieb,"
   in *Allgemeine Deutsche Biographie* 9:566–68 (1879; http://www
   .deutsche-biographie.de/pnd118541374.html?anchor=adb); and
   Elizabeth Karg-Gasterstädt, "Graff, Eberhard Gottlieb," in *Neue
   Deutsche Biographie* 6:730 (http://www.deutsche-biographie.de).

9  Joachim Burkhard Richter, *Hans Ferdinand Maßmann: Altdeutscher
   Patriotismus im 19. Jahrhundert* (Berlin: Walter de Gruyter, 1992).

10 See, in particular, William Roach, "Francisque Michel: A Pioneer in Medieval Studies," *Proceedings of the American Philosophical Society* 114, no. 3 (1970): 168–78; R. Howard Bloch, *A Needle
   in the Right Hand of God: The Norman Conquest of 1066 and the
   Making and Meaning of the Bayeux Tapestry* (New York: Random
   House, 2006), chap. 1.

11 Stephan Müller, *Vom Annolied zur Kaiserchronik: Zu Text-und
   Forschungsgeschichte einer verlorenen deutschen Reimchronik*
   (Heidelberg: Universitätsverlag C. Winter, 1999), 7. Hans-Harald
   Müller considers intellectual controversies in which the living
   attack representative dead scholars in a way that handles them
   as *Untoten* because their ideas continue to have living defenders
   and opponents ("Die Lebendigen und die Untoten: Lassen sich
   Auseinandersetzungen zwischen Wissenschaftskonzeptionen
   als 'Kontroversen' rekonstruieren? Am Beispiel von Positivismus
   und Geistesgeschichte," in *Kontroversen in der Literaturtheorie/
   Literaturtheorie in der Kontroverse*, ed. Ralf Klausnitzer and
   Carlos Spoerhase [Bern: Lang, 2007], 171–82).

12 John Edwin Sandys, *A History of Classical Scholarship* (Cambridge: Cambridge University Press, 1908), 3:241.

13 On the discovery and early history of the manuscript leaves, see
   William Holmes Bennett, *The Gothic Commentary on the Gospel
   of John: Skeireins aiwaggeljons þairh iohannen: A Decipherment,
   Edition, and Translation* (New York: Modern Language Association of America, 1960), 5–11. Some of the fragments remained
   in the Ambrosiana, while others had been taken to the Vatican
   Library by Pope Paul V in 1618.

14 On Árni Magnússon, see Hans Bekker-Nielsen and Ole Widding, *Arne Magnusson, the Manuscript Collector*, trans. Robert W.
Mattila (Odense, Denmark: Odense University Press, 1972). On
the history of Danish manuscript collecting, see Fjalldal, "To
Fall by Ambition."

15 Beowulf, *Klaeber's Beowulf and The Fight at Finnsburg*, ed.
Robert Dennis Fulk, Robert E. Bjork, and John D. Niles, 4th ed.
(Toronto: University of Toronto Press, 2008), xxvi.

16 Bartholomäus [Jernej] Kopitar, *Grammatik der slavischen Sprache
in Krain, Kärnten und Steyermark* (Laibach [Ljubljana], Slovenia:
W. H. Korn, 1808).

17 Merchiers, *Cultural Nationalism in the South Slav Habsburg Lands
in the Early Nineteenth Century*, 172–82.

18 Kopitar explicitly compares his discoveries to those being made
by Mai in *Glagolita Clozianus* (Vienna: Carolus Gerold Bibliopola, 1836), xxxiv.

19 On the discovery of the fragments, see Josef Hahn, *Bartholomäus Kopitar und seine Beziehungen zu München* (Munich:
R. Trofenik, 1982), 135–39.

20 Bernhard Joseph Docen, "Nachrichten von einigen alten
Handschriften der ehemaligen Freysinger Stiftsbibliothek," in
*Beyträge zur Geschichte und Literatur, vorzüglich aus den Schätzen
der pfalzbaierischen Centralbibliothek zu München*, ed. Johann
Christoph Freiherr von Aretin (Munich: In Kommission der
Sehererschen Kunst- und Buchhandlung, 1806), 7:230; Josef
Dobrovský, "Nachricht von drey slawischen Aufsätzen, welche
in einer sehr alten lateinischen Handschrift der öffentlichen
Bibliothek zu München gefunden worden sind," in Josef Do-
brovský: *Slovanka: Zur Kenntniss der alten und neuen slawischen
Literatur, der Sprachkunde nach allen Mundarten, der Geschichte
und Alterthümer* (Prague: In der Herrschen Buchhandlung, 1814),
249–51.

21 "Ich enthalte mich absichtlich aller Erläuterungen, deren diese
schätzbaren Überbleibsel gar sehr bedürfen, da ich gebornen

Krainern nicht vorgreifen will, welche nicht lange mehr säumen werden, diese alten Denkmäler ihre Sprache öffentlich bekannt zu machen und sie mit einem zweckmässigen Commentar zu versehen" (Josef Dobrovský, "Nachricht von drey slawischen Aufsätzen, welche in einer sehr alten lateinischen Handschrift der öffentlichen Bibliothek zu München gefunden worden sind," 251).

22 Merchiers, *Cultural Nationalism in the South Slav Habsburg Lands in the Early Nineteenth Century*, 62.

23 Hahn, *Bartholomäus Kopitar und seine Beziehungen zu München*, 5–6.

24 Petr Keppen, ed., *Sobranie slovenskih pamjatnikov, nahodjaščihsja vně Rossii*. Book. 1 *Pamjatniki sobrannye v Germanii*. (St. Petersburg: Tipografia Imperatorskago vospitatel'nago doma, 1827), 1–27.

25 For a brief introduction to these scholars and their literature, see Christiane Pankow, *Die Wirkung der Deutschen Grammatik von Jacob Grimm auf die grammatischen Ansichten russischer Sprachforscher im 19. Jahrhundert* (Tübingen: G. Narr, 2002), 23–32.

26 Alexandr Khristoforovich Vostokov, "Rassuždenie o slavjanskom jazyke," *Trud obshhestva ljubitelej rossijskoj slovesnosti pri Imperatorskom Moskovskom universitete* 17 (1820): 9–10, 15–27. I wish to acknowledge the assistance of Pavel V. Lukin for his help with this text. On Vostokov's edition, see Merchiers, *Cultural Nationalism in the South Slav Habsburg Lands in the Early Nineteenth Century*, 159, note 101, citing Joep Leerssen.

27 Eberhard Gottlieb Graff, *Diutiska: Denkmäler deutscher Sprache und Literatur aus alten Handschriften*, 3 vols. (Stuttgart: J. G. Cotta'schen Buchhandlung, 1826–29).

28 Eberhard Gottlieb Graff, *Althochdeutscher Sprachschatz, oder: Wörterbuch der althochdeutschen Sprache*, 6 vols. (Berlin: beim Verfasser und in Commission der Nikolaischen Buchhandlung, 1834–42).

29 J. Richter, *Hans Ferdinand Maßmann*, 48.

30 Quoted in ibid., 57.

31 Ibid., 58, referring to Willi Schröder, *Burschenturner im Kampf um Einheit und Freiheit* (Berlin: Sportverlag, 1967).

32 Ibid., 76.

33 Hans Ferdinand Massmann, *Kurze und wahrhaftige Beschreibung des grossen Burschenfestes auf der Wartburg bei Eisenach am 18ten und 19ten Siegesmonds 1817* (Jena: Frommann, 1817).

34 "Muttersprache und Vaterlandeskunde in größten Umfange des Germanenthums" (quoted in J. Richter, *Hans Ferdinand Maßmann*, 84).

35 On Massmann's bitter conflict with Hoffmann over the *Kaiserchronik*, see S. Müller, *Vom Annolied zur Kaiserchronik*.

36 J. Richter, *Hans Ferdinand Maßmann*, 150–51.

37 Ibid., 153; S. Müller, *Vom Annolied zur Kaiserchronik*, 17–18. Nevertheless, as Müller and Richter point out, Massmann did later receive some support from the presidents of the Gesellschaft, Georg Heinrich Pertz and Johann Friedrich Böhmer.

38 Bartholomäus Kopitar, B. *Kopitars Briefwechsel mit Jakob Grimm*, ed. Max Vasmer (Vienna: Böhlau, 1987), 124.

39 Hans Ferdinand Massmann, ed., *Skeireins aiwaggeljons þairh ïohannen, Auslegung des Evangelii Johannis in gothischer Sprache. Aus römischen und mayländischen Handschriften nebst lateinischer Uebersetzung, belegenden Anmerkungen, geschichtlicher Untersuchung, gothisch-lateinischem Wörterbuche und Schriftproben. Im Auftrage Seiner Königlichen Hoheit des Kronprinzen Maximilian von Bayern erlesen, erläutert und zum ersten Male herausgegeben* (Munich: Verlag von George Jaquet, 1834).

40 "Deutschland, Vor allem Oberdeutschland und Bayern, wegen Verwandtschaft der Mundart, gebührt es, in würdiger und wißenschaftlicher vollendeter Gestalte die ältesten Denkmale seiner Ursprache, jenes gothische Bibelwerk des 4. bis 6ten Jahrhunderts endlich zu Einem Ganzen vereinigt zu Tage zu fördern" (ibid., vii–viii).

41 "Sieger und Besiegte hätten sich leicht gemischt; nicht so sitten-kräftige Germanen mit entarteten Romanen. Die 'arianischen' Gothen erhielten und bildeten in Griechenland und Welschland ihr selbständiges Volksleben aus, sie vermischen weder Sitte, noch Sprache" (ibid., 110).

42 See, in particular, Roach, "Francisque Michel"; Bloch, *A Needle in the Right Hand of God*, chap. 1. On interest in the Roland legend in France prior to the discovery of Digby 23, discussed below, and in particular on the manner in which nineteenth-century national aspirations continue to shape assumptions about the manuscript and the text it contains, see Andrew Taylor, "Was There a Song of Roland?," *Speculum* 76, no. 1 (2001): 28–65.

43 Among the voluminous works on Guizot, see Robert Legrand, *Guizot et son temps: propos et portraits* (Abbeville, France: F. Paillart, 2002); Marina Valensise, ed. *François Guizot et la culture politique de son temps: colloque de la Fondation Guizot-Val Richer* (Paris: Gallimard and Le Seuil, 1991).

44 Thomas Tyrwhitt, *The Canterbury Tales of Chaucer: To Which Are Added an Essay upon His Language and Versification, an Introductory Discourse, and Notes*, 4 vols. (London: T. Payne, 1775–78).

45 Gervais de la Rue, *Essais historiques sur les bardes, les jongleurs et les trouvères normands et anglo-normands, suivis de pièces de Malherbe, qu'on ne trouve dans aucune édition de ses oeuvres* (Caen, France: Mancel, 1834), 2:57–65. Francisque Michel graciously acknowledged both of these earlier scholars in his introduction.

46 Shippey, "The Case of Beowulf," 228.

47 Ibid., 229–31. The text is conveniently translated in Shippey and Haarder, eds., *Beowulf: The Critical Heritage*, 123–31.

48 Kopitar, *Glagolita Clozianus*, xxxv–xli.

49 On Kopitar's Pannonian-Slovenian theories, see Merchiers, *Cultural Nationalism in the South Slav Habsburg Lands in the Early Nineteenth Century*, 60–65.

50 On the problem posed to theories of the *Chanson de Roland* as a national epic by the fact that the Oxford version is in Anglo-Norman and presumably created for an Anglo-Norman audience in England, see Taylor, "Was There a Song of Roland?," 49–53.

51 "Das Rolandslied, in welchem sich die deutschen Namen der Helden noch zum Theil erhalten haben, mag wohl in frühester Zeit auch in fränkischer Sprache gesungen worden sein, und ist erst nach ihrem Verschwinden der romanischen Poesie aufschließlich zugefallen. Mit recht hat Uhland die Ansicht geäußert, daß in dem strengen Ernst und in der Derbheit der fränkischen Heldensage der deutsche Geist, aus dem sie hervorgegangen sey noch durchleuchte " (Wilhelm Grimm, introduction to *Ruolandes Liet* [Göttingen: Verlag der Dieterichischen Buchhandlung, 1838], cxx).

52 Francisque Michel, *Bibliothèque Anglo-Saxonne* (Paris: Silvestre, 1837).

53 Francisque Michel, *Anglo-Norman Poem on the Conquest of Ireland* (London: William Pickering, 1837).

54 Wace, *Le Roman de Rou*, ed. A. J. Holden (Paris: Éditions A. and J. Picard, 1971), 2:183, lines 8017–19.

55 "Vers Engletere passait il la mer salse, / Ad oes seint Pere en cunquist le chevage."

56 Quoted in *La Chanson de Roland—The Song of Roland: The French Corpus*, ed. Joseph J. Duggan (Turnhout, Belgium: Brepols, 2006), 7.

57 Francisque Michel, *Chanson de Roland ou de Roncevaux* (Paris: Chez Silvestre, 1837), xi–xii.

58 *La Chanson de Roland*, ed. Duggan, 7.

59 Quoted in ibid., 8.

60 See the list of his publications provided as an appendix to Roach, "Francisque Michel," 173–78.

61 On attempts to date Beowulf, see, most recently, Roberta Frank, "A Scandal in Toronto: The Dating of Beowulf a Quarter Century On," *Speculum* 82, no. 4 (2007): 843–64.

62 For a modern evaluation of the text, see Knut Schäferdiek, "Die Fragmente der 'Skeireins' und der Johanneskommentar des Theodor von Herakleia," in Knut Schäferdiek, *Schwellenzeit: Beiträge zur Geschichte des Christentums in Spätantike und Frühmittelalter* (Berlin: Walter de Gruyter, 1996), 83.

63 See especially the new edition, *Brižinski spomeniki: Znanstvenokritična izdaja*, ed. Jože Faganel et al. (Ljubljana, Slovenia: Znanstvenoraziskovalni center SAZU, Inštitut za slovensko literaturo in literarne vede, 1993). And see Janko Kos, et al., eds., *Zbornik Brižinski spomeniki* (Ljubljana, Slovenia: Znanstvenoraziskovalni center SAZU, Inštitut za slovensko literaturo in literarne vede, 1996).

## 2. RELIGION AND LANGUAGE

1 Erich Auerbach, *Literary Language and Its Public in Late Latin Antiquity and in the Middle Ages*, trans. Ralph Manheim (New York: Pantheon, 1965), especially 25–66.

2 Dennis Brown, *Vir Trilinguis: A Study in the Biblical Exegesis of Saint Jerome* (Kampen, the Netherlands: Kok Pharos, 1992), especially chap. 3, "Jerome and the Hebraica Veritas."

3 "Neque enim usque adeo teipsum oblivisci potuisses, ut homo Afer scribens Afris, cum simus utrique in Africa constituti, Punica nomina exagitanda existimares. . . . Quae lingua si improbatur abs te, nega Punicis libris, ut a viris doctissimis proditur, multa sapienter esse mandata memoriae. Poeniteat te certe ibi natum, ubi hujus linguae cunabula recalent" (Augustine, *S. Aurelii Augustini Operum Sectio II S. Augustini Epistulae, Corpus scriptorum ecclesiasticorum latinorum [CSEL]*, vol. 34, ed. Alois Goldbacher [Vienna: F. Tempsky, 1895], 41. See also James Noel Adams, *Bilingualism and the Latin Language* (Cambridge: Cambridge University Press, 2003), 239.

4 "Punica lingua esset instructus" (Augustine, *S. Aurelii Augustini Operum Sectio II S. Augustini Epistulae*, 57:348). See also Adams,

*Bilingualism and the Latin Language*, 238. On Augustine's problems with Fussala, where he installed a young man whose primary qualification seems to have been his knowledge of Punic and who soon became a petty tyrant, see James Joseph O'Donnell, *Augustine: A New Biography* (New York: Harper-Collins, 2005), 246.

5 Jerome, *Sancti Eudebii Hieronymi epistulae I, Corpus scriptorum ecclesiasticorum latinorum (CSEL)*, vol. 54, ed. Isidor Hilberg (Vienna: F. Tempsky, 1910), 71–72.

6 "Plane times, ne eloquentissimus homo in Syro sermone vel Graeco ecclesias circumeam, populos seducam, scisma conficiam" (quoted in Adams, *Bilingualism and the Latin Language*, 269). See D. Brown, *Vir Trilinguis*, 71–82.

7 Of course, in the contemporary polemic, orthodox theologians such as Salvian argued that heretics, including the Arian Goths and Vandals, were deficient because they did not have all of the scriptures, and moreover they understood the scriptures in a heretical manner. Salvian maintained that for him and other Orthodox Christians, on the other hand, "nos . . . tantum scripturas sacras plenas inviolatas, integras habemus . . . nos tantummodo bene legimus" (*De gubernatione Dei, Libri VIII*, ed. Carolus Halm, *MGH Auctores Antiquissimi* 1, 1 [Berlin: Weidmann, 1877], 56). See Walter Henss, "Die Integrität der Bibelübersetzung im religiösen Denken des 5. Jahrhunderts," in *The Bible and Medieval Culture*, ed. Willem Lourdaux and Daniël Verhelst (Leuven, Belgium: Leuven University Press 1970), 36.

8 Cassiodorus, "De institutione divinarum litterarum, I, 15," in Cassiodorus, *Cassiodori senatoris Institutiones*, ed. Roger Aubrey Baskerville Mynors (Oxford: Clarendon Press of Oxford University Press, 1937), 41–51.

9 "Audiat Spiritus sanctus sincerissima quae donavit, recipiat ille beata quae contulit" (ibid., 48).

10 On the characteristics of biblical Latin manuscripts prior to the Carolingian reform, see Jean Gribomont and Jean Mallet, "Le

latin biblique aux mains des barbares: Les manuscrits UEST des Prophètes," *Romanobarbarica* 4 (1979): 35–105.

11  On the vast literature of reform of Latin in the Carolingian period, see Michel Banniard, "Théorie et pratique de la langue et du style chez Alcuin: Rusticité feinte et rusticité masquée," *Francia* 13 (1986): 579–601; Michel Banniard, *Viva voce: Communication écrite et communication orale du IVe au IXe siècle en Occident latin* (Paris: Institut des études augustiniennes, 1992); Roger Wright, ed., *Latin and the Romance Languages in the Early Middle Ages* (London: Routledge, 1991); Roger Wright, "La période de transition du latin, de la lingua Romana et du français," *Médiévales* 45 (2003): 11–23; Roger Wright, "Translation between Latin and Romance in the Early Middle Ages," in *Translation Theory and Practice in the Middle Ages*, ed. Jeanette Beer, (Kalamazoo: Medieval Institute Publications, Western Michigan University, 1997), 7–32; Roger Wright, *Late Latin and Early Romance in Spain and Carolingian France* (Liverpool: Cairns, 1982), 118–20. See also Michel Banniard and Marc Van Uytfanghe, "Consciousness of a Linguistic Dichotomy in Carolingian Gaul," in *Latin and the Romance Languages in the Early Middle Ages*, ed. Roger Wright (London: Routledge, 1991), 114–29; Michèle Goyens and Werner Verbeke, eds., *The Dawn of the Written Vernacular in Western Europe* (Leuven, Belgium: Leuven University Press, 2003); Marieke van Acker, Rika van Deyck, and Marc van Uytfanghe, eds. *Latin écrit—roman oral? De la dichotomisation à la continuité, Corpus Christianorum, Lingua Patrum*, 5 (Turnhout, Belgium: Brepols, 2008).

12  "Ut nullus credat, quod nonnisi in tribus linguis Deus orandus sit, quia in omni lingua Deus adoratur et homo exauditur, si iusta petierit" (*Concilium Francofurtense*, ed. Albert Wermminghoff, *MGH Concilia*, 2, part 1 [Hanover: Hahn, 1906], 171. See Michael Richter, "Concept and Evolution of the *Tres linguae sacrae*," in *Language of Religion, Language of the People: Medieval Judaism, Christianity, and Islam*, ed. Ernst Bremer, Jörg Jarnut,

Michael Richter, and David Wasserstein. (Munich: Wilhelm Fink Verlag, 2006), 15–23.

13 "Et fidelium fratrum relatione didicimus, apud quasdam Scytharum gentes manxime Thomitanos eadem locutione, divina hactenus celebrari officia" (Walafrid Strabo, *Walahfrid Strabo libellus de exordiis et incrementis quarundam in observationibus ecclesiasticis rerum*, ed. and trans. Alice L. Harting-Correa [Leiden: Brill, 1996] 1:7). See Herwig Wolfram, *Gotische Studien: Volk und Herrschaft im frühen Mittelalter* (Munich: Beck, 2005), 240, note 30.

14 Stephan Endlicher and August Henirch Hoffmann von Fallersleben, *Fragmenta theodisca versionis antiquissimae evangelii S. Mathaei et aliquot homilliarum. E membranis Monseensibus Bibliothecae Palatinae Vindobonensis* (Vienna: Typis Caroli Gerold, 1834). On Endlicher, see Helmut Dolezal, "Endlicher, Stephan Ladislaus," in *Neue Deutsche Biographie* (1959; http://www.deutsche-biographie.de/pnd100122434.html).

15 Elke Krotz, "Hear saget fona gotspelle Zur äußeren und inneren Kohärenz einer lateinisch-althochdeutschen Sammelhandschrift," in *Volkssprachig-lateinische Mischtexte und Textensembles in der althochdeutschen, altsächsischen und altenglischen Überlieferung: Mediävistisches Kolloquium des Zentrums für Mittelalterstudien der Otto-Friedrich-Universität Bamberg am 16. und 17. November 2001*, ed. Rolf Bergmann (Heidelberg: Universitätsverlag, 2003), 175–86.

16 See Peter Štih, "Slowenisch, Alpenslawisch oder Slawisch: zwischen Donau und Adria im Frühmittelalter," in *Sprache und Identität im frühen Mittelalter*, ed. Walter Pohl and Bernhard Zeller (Vienna: Verlag der Österreichen Akademie der Wissenschaften, 2012), 171–83.

17 "Juvenci, Aratoris, Prudentii caeterorumque multorum, qui sua lingua dicta et miracula Christi decenter ornabant; nos vero, quamvis eadem fide eademque gratia instructi, divinorum verborum splendorem clarissimum proferre propria lingua

dicebant pigrescere" (Otfrid of Weissenburg, *Otfrids Evangelienbuch*, ed. Oskar Erdman, 4th ed. revised by Ludwig Wolff [Tübingen: Niemeyer, 1962], 4).

18 "Qui in illis alienae linguae difficultatem horrescit, hic propria lingua cognoscat sanctissima verba, deique legem sua lingua intelligens, inde se vel parum quid deviare mente propria pertimescat" (ibid.).

19 Hafs ibn Albar al Quti, *Le psautier mozarabe de Hafs le Goth*, ed. and trans. Marie Thérèse Urvoy (Toulouse: Presses universitaires du Mirail, 1994), 3. I am grateful to Michael Cooperson for his assistance with the Arabic translation. See also Ann Christys, "How Can I Trust You, Since You Are a Christian and I Am a Moor?," in *Texts and Identities in the Early Middle Ages*, ed. Richard Corradini, Rob Meens, Christina Pössel, and Philip Shaw (Vienna: Verlag der Österreichischer Akademie der Wissenschaften, 2006), 359–72, especially 360–61.

20 Alfred of Wessex, *King Alfred's West-Saxon Version of Gregory's Pastoral Care*, ed. Henry Sweet (London: N. Trübner, 1871–72), 5–6. See also Kathleen Davis, "The Performance of Translation Theory in King Alfred's National Literary Program," in *Manuscript, Narrative, Lexicon: Essays on Literary and Cultural Transmission in Honor of Whitney F. Bolton*, ed. Robert Boenig and Kathleen Davis (Lewisburg, PA: Bucknell University Press, 2000), 154; Nicole Guenther Discenza, "Alfred's Verse Preface to the Pastoral Care and the Chain of Authority," *Neophilologus* 84, no. 4 (2001): 625–33; Malcolm Godden, "The Alfredian Project and Its Aftermath: Rethinking the Literary History of the Ninth and Tenth Centuries," *Proceedings of the British Academy* 162 (2009): 93–122, especially 100–107.

21 James Hurt, *Ælfric* (New York: Twayne, 1972), 84–103.

22 Albert S. Cook and Chauncey B. Tinker, trans., *Select Translations from Old English Prose* (Boston: Ginn, 1908), 150–51. The original is: "Nu þincð me, leof, þæt þæt weorc is swiðe pleolic me oððe ænigum men to underbeginnenne, for þan þe ic

ondræde, gif sum dysig man þas boc ræt oððe rædan g<e>hyrþ
þæt he wille wenan, þæt he mote lybban nu on þære niw<an>
æ, swa swa þa ealdan fæderas leofodon þa on þære tide, ær þan
þe seo ealde æ gesett wære, oþþe swa swa men leofodon under
Moyses æ. Hwilon ic wiste þæt sum mæssepreost, se þe min
magister wæs on þam timan, hæfde þa boc Genesis, and he cuðe
be dæle Lyden understandan: þa cwæþ he be þam heahfædere
Iacobe, þæt he hæfde feower wif, twa geswustra and heora
twa þinena. Ful soð he sæde, ac he nyste, ne ic þa git, hu micel
todal ys betweohx þære ealdan æ and þære niwan" (Ælfric, *The
Old English Version of the Heptateuch, Ælfric's Treatise on the Old
and New Testament and His Preface to Genesis*, ed. S. J. Crawford,
reprint of 1922 ed. [Oxford: Oxford University Press, 1969], 76).

23  Renée R. Trilling, *The Aesthetics of Nostalgia: Historical Representation in Old English Verse* (Toronto: University of Toronto Press,
2009), especially 67–68.

24  Hafs ibn Albar al Quti, *Le psautier mozarabe de Hafs le Goth*, 19,
lines 117–19.

25  "Litteras denique Sclaviniscas a Constantino quondam philoso-
pho reppertas, quibus Deo laudes debite resonent, iure lauda-
mus et in eadem lingua Christi domini nostri preconia et opera
enarrentur, iubemus; neque enim tribus tantum, sed omnibus
linguis Dominum laudare auctoritate sacra monemur, quę
pręcipit dicens: 'Laudate Dominum omnes gentes et collaudate
eum omnes populi,' et apostoli repleti Spiritu sancto locuti sunt
omnibus linguis magnalia Dei; hinc et Paulus cęlestis quoque
tuba insonat a monens: 'Omnis lingua confiteatur, quia dominus
noster Iesus Christus in gloria est Dei Patris'; de quibus etiam
linguis in prima ad Corinthios epistola satis et manifeste nos
ammonet, quatenus linguis loquentes ecclesiam Dei ędificemus.
Nec sane fidei vel doctrinę aliquid obstat sive missas in eadem
Sclavinica lingua canere sive sacrum evangelium vel lectiones
divinas novi et veteris testamenti bene translatas et interpre-
tatas legere aut alia horarum officia omnia psallere, quoniam,

qui fecit tres linguas principales, Hebream scilicet Grecam et Latinam, ipse creavit et alias omnes ad laudem et gloriam suam. Iubemus tamen, ut in omnibus ecclesiis terrę vestrę propter maiorem honorificentiam evangelium Latine legatur et postmodum Sclavinica linguą translatum in auribus populi Latina verba non intellegentis adnuntietur, sicut in quibusdam ecclesiis fieri videtur; et, si tibi et iudicibus tuis placet missas Latina lingua magis audire, precipimus, ut Latine missarum tibi sollemnia celebrentur" (John VIII, *Regestum Iohannes VIII. Papae*, ed. Erich Caspar, *MGH Epistolae* 7 [Berlin: Weidmann, 1928], 223–24.)

26 "Divina autem officia et sacra mysteria ac missarum solemnia quae idem Methodius Sclavorum lingua celebrare praesumpsit, quod ne ulterius faceret supra sacratissimum beati Petri corpus iuramento firmaverat, sui perjurii reatum perhorrescentes nullo modo deinceps a quolibet praesumatur. Dei namque nostraque apostolica auctoritate sub anathematis vinculo interdicimus, excepto quod ad simplicis populi et non intelligentis aedificationem attinet, si Evangelii, vel apostoli, expositio ab eruditis eadem lingua annuntietur, et largimur et exhortamur, et ut frequentissime fiat monemus, ut omnis lingua laudet Deum, et confiteatur ei" (Stephanus V, *Epistola ad Zuentopolcum regem*, *Patrologia Latina* 129, col. 804).

27 *Historia Salonitana Maior*, ed. Nada Klaić, (Belgrade: Naučno delo, 1967), 95–104. See also John A. V. Fine Jr., *The Early Medieval Balkans: A Critical Survey from the Sixth to the Late Twelfth Century* (Ann Arbor: University of Michigan Press, 1991), 267–81.

28 "Ita ut secundum mores sancta romane ecclesie Sclavinorum terra ministerium sacrificii peragant in latina scilicet lingua, non autem in extranea. Quia nullus filius aliquid loqui debet vel sapere, nisi ut pater ei insinuaverit. Et quia Sclavi specialissimi filii sanctae romane ecclesie sunt, in doctrina matris permanere debent " (*Historia Salonitana Maior*, 96).

29 "Inter que siquidem hoc firmatum est et statutum, ut nullus de cetero in lingua Sclavonica presumeret divina misteria celebrare,

nisi tantum in Latina et Greca, nec aliquis eiusdem lingue promoveretur ad sacros" (Thomas of Split, *Archdeacon Thomas of Split, History of the Bishops of Salona and Split*, Latin text ed. and trans. Olga Pereć, Damir Karbić, Mirjana Matijević Sokol, and James Ross Sweeney [Budapest: Central European Press, 2006], 78). On Thomas, see Mirjana Matijević Sokol, "Archdeacon Thomas of Split (1200–1268): A Source of Early Croatian History," *Review of Croatian History* 3, no. 1 (2007): 251–70.

30 "Dicebant enim, Goticas litteras a quodam Methodio heretico fuisse repertas, qui multa contra catholice fidei normam in eadem Sclavonica lingua mentiendo conscripsit" (Thomas of Split , *Archdeacon Thomas of Split*, 79).

31 Ibid., 77, note 4.

32 Gregory VII, *Das Register Gregors*, , ed. Erich. Caspar, *MGH Epistolae Selectae* 2 (Berlin: Weidmann, 1923), 473–74.

33 "Ex hoc nempe saepe volventibus liquet non immerito sacram Scripturam omnipotenti Deo placuisse quibusdam locis esse occultam, ne, si ad liquidum cunctis pateret, forte vilesceret et subjaceret despectui, aut prave intellecta a mediocribus in errorem induceret" (ibid., 474).

34 Herbert Edward John Cowdery, "Pope Gregory VII (1073–85) and the Liturgy,"*Journal of Theological Studies*, n.s., 55, no. 1 (2004): 78.

35 "Preterea notum vobis fieri volumus , quod nobis quidem tacere non est liberum, vobis autem non solum ad futuram, sed etiam ad presentem gloriam valde necessarium , videlicet regnum Hyspanię ex antiquis constitutionibus beato PETRO et sanctę Romanę ecclesię in ius et proprietatem esse traditum" (Gregory VII, *Das Register Gregors*, 345–46).

36 "Decretum, in his curiis fuit, ut privilegia vulgariter, conscribantur, quia Latinitatis difficultas errores et dubia maxima pariebat et laycos decipiebat" (Iohannes Victoriensis, *Liber Certarum historiarum, Book. II*, rec. A, in *MGH Scriptores rerum Germanicarum*

*in usum scholarum separatim editi 36/1*, ed. Fedor Schneider .
[Hanover: Hahn, 1910], 221).

## 3. VERNACULAR LANGUAGE AND SECULAR POWER IN EMERGING EUROPE

1 "La résistible ascension des vulgaires. Contacts entre latin et langues vulgaires au bas Moyen Âge. Problèmes pour l'historien." *Mélanges de l'École française de Rome—Moyen Âge* 117, no. 2 (2005).

2 Serge Lusignan, *La langue des rois au Moyen Âge: Le français en France et en Angleterre* (Paris: Presses universitaires de France, 2004).

3 Thomas Brunner, "Le passage aux langues vernaculaires dans les actes de la pratique en Occident," *Le Moyen Âge* 115 (2009): 29–72.

4 Jérôme Belmon and Françoise Vielliard, "Latin farci et occitan dans les actes du XIe siècle," *Pratiques de l'écrit documentaire au XIe siècle* 155 (1997): 149–83; David Trotter, "'Si le français n'y peut aller': Villers-Cotterêts and Mixed-Language Documents from the Pyrenees," in *Conceptions of Europe in Renaissance France*, ed. David Cowling (Amsterdam: Rodopi, 2006), 81; Brunner, "Le passage aux langues vernaculaires dans les actes de la pratique en Occident," 34–35.

5 Brunner, "Le passage aux langues vernaculaires dans les actes de la pratique en Occident," 61.

6 Ottokar, "Ottokars Österreichische Reimchronik," ed. Joseph Seemüller, *MGH Deutsche Chroniken* 5, part 1 (Hanover, 1890), 173–74, lines 13067–186. On this text and its relationship to other anecdotes concerning Rudolf and his social and cultural status, see Herwig Wolfram, "Meinungsbildung und Propaganda im österreichischen Mittelalter," in *Öffentliche Meinung in der Geschichte Österreichs*, ed. Erich Zöllner (Vienna, Österreichische Bundesverlag 1979), 19.

7 See chapter 2, note 36. On this text and the complex issue of the vernacular and Latin in the Habsburg court of the thirteenth century in general, see Alphons Lhotsky, "Zur Frühgeschichte der Wiener Hofbibliothek," in *Europäisches Mittelalter: Das Land Österreich*, vol. 1 of *Aufsätze und Vorträge*, ed. Hans Wagner and Heinrich Koller. (Munich: Oldenbourg, 1970), 149–93, especially 158–67. Lhotsky argues that "die lateinische Sprache war im 13. Jahrhundert wirklich nicht mehr ohne weiteres in der Lage, alltägliches mit der nötigen klaren Eindeutigkeit auszudrücken" (161).

8 Rudolf-Dieter Heim, *Romanen und Germanen in Charlemagnes Reich: Untersuchungen zur Benennung romanischer und germanischer Völker, Sprache und Länder in französischen Dichtungen des Mittelalters* (Munich: Fink, 1984), 24.

9 Irenaeus of Lyon, *Adversus Haerese Irénée de Lyon, Contre les hérésies*, ed. Adelin Rousseau and Louis Doutreleau (Paris: Cerf, 1979), 2:25.

10 Sidonius Apollinaris, "Epistulae 4.17," in *Lettres (Livres I–V)*, vol. 2 of *Sidoine Apollinaire*, ed. André Loyen (Paris: Belles Lettres, 1970), 149–50. See Guy Halsall, *Barbarian Migrations and the Roman West 367–568* (Cambridge: Cambridge University Press, 2008), 496.

11 "Sic barbarorum familiaris, quod tamen nescius barbarismorum, par ducibus antiquis lingua manuque, sed quorum dextra solebat non stilum minus tractare quam gladium. Quocirca sermonis pompa Romani, si qua adjuc uspiam est, Belgicis olim sive Rhenanis abolita terris in te resedit, quo vel incolumi vel perorante, etsi apud limitem ipsum Latina iura ceciderunt verba non titubant" (Sidonius Apollinaris, "Epistulae 4.17," 149–50).

12 "Aestimari minime potest, quanto mihi ceterisque sit risui, quotiens audio, quod te praesente formidet linguae suae facere barbarus barbarismum. Adstupet tibi epistulas interpretanti curva Germanorum senectus et negotiis mutuis arbitrum discepatoremque desumit" (Sidonius Apollinaris, "Epistulae 5.5," in

*Lettres (Livres I–V)*, vol. 2 of *Sidoine Apollinaire*, ed. André Loyen [Paris: Belles Lettres, 1970], 180–81).

13  The best discussion of the role of education in making the elite remains Peter Brown, *Power and Persuasion in Late Antiquity: Towards a Christian Empire* (Madison: University of Wisconsin Press, 1992).

14  Cassiodorus, *Cassiodori Senatoris Variae*, ed. Theodor Mommsen, *MGH Auctores antiquissimi*, 12 (Berlin: Weidmann, 1894), Var. 5, 40, 166–67.

15  "Pueri stirpis Romanae nostra lingua loquuntur, eximie indicantes exhibere se nobis futuram fidem, quorum iam videntur affectasse sermonem" (ibid., Var. 8, 21, 253). On Cyprianus and his family, see Patrick Amory, *People and Identity in Ostrogothic Italy, 489–554* (Cambridge: Cambridge University Press, 2004), 153–55. Cyprianus may have thus found favor with the Gothic kings, but his role as principal accuser of Boethius suggests that within post-Roman society, Roman suspicions of careerists who learned the language of their barbarian lords had a certain basis. James O'Donnell comments on Cyprianus and "his whole rather distasteful family" in *Cassiodorus* (Berkeley: University of California Press, 1979; post print 1995, http://www9.george town.edu/faculty/jod/texts/cassbook/toc.html, accessed January 21, 2009). They may have been distasteful to their Romanizing opponents and modern scholars, but they obviously weren't to the Gothic rulers of Italy.

16  For a general introduction to social linguistics in England, see Tim William Machan, *English in the Middle Ages*, (Oxford: Oxford University Press, 2003).

17  Regina Maria Dröll, "Sprachwahl als Indikator politischer Standortbestimmung im 'deutschen' Mittelalter: Der Umgang mit der Volkssprache von den Karolingern zu den Staufern," PhD diss., Johann Wolfgang Goethe Universität, 2005.

18  In addition to the works of Wright and Banniard cited above (see note 11 in chapter 2), see Roger Wright, "Linguistic and

Ethnic Identities in the Iberian Peninsula (400–1000 A.D.)," in *Sprache und Identität im frühen Mittelalter*, ed. Walter Pohl and Bernhard Zeller (Vienna: Verlag der Österreichen Akademien der Wissenschaften, 2012), 99–108; Michel Banniard, "Acrolecte et identité culturelle en Francia carolingienne (VIIIe–IXe s.)," in *Sprache und Identität im frühen Mittelalter*, 109–20.

19 Mayke de Jong, "Some Reflections on Mandarin Language," in *East and West: Modes of Communication*, ed. Euangelos Chrysos and Ian Wood (Leiden: Brill, 1999), 61–69.

20 *Concilium Turonense anno 813, Concilia Aevi Karolini* ed. Albert Werminghoff, *MGH Concilia*, 2, part 1 (Hanover: Hahn, 1905), 288. Michel Banniard argues that the canon, which ordered "et ut easdem omelias quisque aperte transferre studeat in rusticam Romanam linguam aut Thiotiscam, quo facilius cuncti possint intelligere quae dicuntur," uses "transferre" in the sense of translate, not simply transpose into a different register (*Viva voce: Communication écrite et communication orale du IVe au IXe siècle en Occident latin* [Paris: Institut des études augustiniennes, 1992], 411).

21 Franz Bäuml, "Medieval Texts and the Two Theories of Oral-Formulaic Composition: A Proposal for a Third Theory," *New Literary History* 16 (1984–85): 43. See the discussion by Ursula Schaefer, *Vokalität: Altenglische Dichtung zwischen Mündlichkeit und Schriftlichkeit* (Tübingen: Narr, 1992), 115–16, note 49.

22 "Hamelburger Markbeschreibung," in *Althochdeutsches Lesebuch*, ed. Wilhelm Braune and Karl Helm, 16th ed., revised by Ernst A. Ebbinghaus (Tübingen: Max Niemeyer Verlag, 1979), 6; "Würzburger Markebeschreibung," in ibid., 6–8. On the texts, see Ruth Schmidt-Wiegand, "Hammelburger Markbeschreibungen," in *Die deutsche Literatur des Mittelalters: Verfasserlexikon*, ed. Kurt Ruh et al. (Berlin: Walter de Gruyter, 1981), 3:427–28; Ruth Schmidt-Wiegand, "Würzburger Markbeschreibungen," in ibid., 10:1455–58. See also Patrick J. Geary, "Land, Language and

Memory in Europe 700–1100," *Transactions of the Royal Historical Society* 6th series, 9 (1999): 169–84.

23 See Dröll, "Sprachwahl als Indikator politischer Standortbestimmung im 'deutschen' Mittelalter," 63–66.

24 "Hamelburger Markbeschreibung," 6.

25 The procedure by which the boundaries were established is explained in the text: "In nomine domini nostri Ihesu Christi. Notum sit omnibus sanctae dei ecclesiae fidelibus, qualiter Eburhardus missus domni nostri Karoli excellentissimi regis cum omnibus obtimatibus et sensibus istius provinciae in occidentali parte fluvii nomine Moin marcham Uuirziburgarensium, iuste discernendo et ius iurantibus illis subter scriptis optimatibus et senibus circumduxit. Incipientes igitur in loco qui dicitur Otuuinesbrunno, danân in daz haganîna sol, danân in Herostat in den uuîdînen sêo, danân in mittan Nottenlôh, danân in Scelenhouc. Isti sunt qui in his suprascriptis circumduxerunt et iuramento firmaverunt: Zótan Ephfo Landtolt Sigiuuin Runzolf Diotmâr Artumâr Eburraat Hiltuuin Eburkar Gêrmunt Árberaht Folegêr Theotgêr Theodolt" ("Würzburger Markebeschreibung," 6–7).

26 On English boundary clauses, see Kathryn A. Lowe, "The Development of the Anglo-Saxon Boundary Clause," *Nomina* 21 (1998): 63–100.

27 Hannah Vollrath, "Rechtstexte in der oralen Rechtskultur des früheren Mittelalters," in *Mittelalterforschung nach der Wende 1989*, ed. Michael Borgolte (Munich: R. Oldenbourg Verlag, 1995), 329.

28 Mark Rabuck, "The Imagined Boundary: Borders and Frontiers in Anglo-Saxon England," PhD diss., Yale University, 1996, 149–65.

29 The literature on the oaths of Strasbourg is voluminous. See, in particular, Francesco Lo Monaco and Claudia Villa, eds., *I giuramenti di Strasburgo: Testi e tradizione / The Strasbourg Oaths:*

*Texts and Transmission* (Florence: Sismel Edizioni del Galluzzo, 2009), especially the bibliography. On the role of the oaths in the nineteenth century, see John E. Joseph, "842, 1871 and All That: Alsace-Lorraine and the Transformations of Linguistic Nationalism," in *The French Language and Questions of Identity*, ed. Wendy Ayres-Bennett and Mari C. Jones (London: Legenda, 2007), 44–52; R. Howard Bloch, "The First Document and the Birth of Medieval Studies," in *A New History of French Literature*, ed. Denis Hollier (Cambridge: Harvard University Press, 1989), 6–13.

30 Julius Brakelmann, "Die Nithardhandschrift und die Eide von Strassburg," *Zeitschrift für deutsche Philologie* 3 (1871): 85–94. For information on Brakelmann and the history of the rediscovery of the Nithard manuscript, I am grateful to Courtney M. Booker, who treats the matter in "History, Identity, and the First French Text: Nithard's *Historiae* and the Politics of Value," paper presented at the annual meeting of the American Historical Association, New York, 4 January 2009.

31 Rosamond McKitterick, ed., *The New Cambridge Medieval History*, Vol. 2, *c. 700–c. 900* (Cambridge: Cambridge University Press, 1995), 11–12; Rosamond McKitterick, "Latin and Romance: An Historian's Perspective," in *Latin and the Romance Languages in the Early Middle Ages*, ed. Roger Wright (London: Routledge, 1991), 130–45; and Janet L. Nelson, "Public Histories and Private History in the Work of Nithard," *Speculum* 60, no. 2 (1985): 251–93, especially 265–67.

32 "Quoniam vos de nostra stabili fide ac firma fraternitate dubitare credimus." Nithard, *Historiarum Libri III*, 3,5, in *MGH Scriptores rerum Germanicarum in usum scholarum separatim editi* 44, ed. Ernest Müller (Hanover: Hahn, 1907), 35.

33 See especially Gerd Althoff, *Spielregeln der Politik im Mittelalter: Kommunikation in Frieden und Fehde* (Darmstadt: Primus, 1997).

34 For a detailed discussion of the Koblenz oaths, see Patrick J. Geary, "Oathtaking and Conflict Management in the Ninth

Century," in *Rechtsverständnis und Handlungsstrategien im mittelalterlichen Konfliktaustrag: Festschrift für Hanna Vollrath*, ed. Stefan Esders and Christine Reinle (Munich: Böhlau, 2007), 239–53.

35  *Capitularia Regum Francorum II*, 1, ed. Alfred Boretius and Victor Krause (Hanover, 1939), no. 242, 153–58.

36  Otfrid of Weissenburg, *Otfrids Evangelienbuch*, ed. Oskar Erdman, 4th ed. revised by Ludwig Wolff (Tübingen: Niemeyer, 1962). On the place of Otfrid's work within a complex cultural context, rather than simply as a manifestation of political Frankish identity encouraged by Louis the German, see Hans J. Hummer, *Politics and Power in Early Medieval Europe* (Cambridge: Cambridge University Press, 2005), especially 130–54.

# Bibliography

PRIMARY SOURCES

Ælfric. *The Old English Version of the Heptateuch, Ælfric's Treatise on the Old and New Testament and His Preface to Genesis.* Edited by S. J. Crawford. Reprint of 1922 ed. Oxford: Oxford University Press, 1969.

Alfred of Wessex. *King Alfred's West-Saxon Version of Gregory's Pastoral Care.* Edited by Henry Sweet. London: N. Trübner, 1871–72.

Augustine. *S. Aurelii Augustini Operum Sectio II S. Augustini Epistulae, Corpus scriptorum ecclesiasticorum latinorum (CSEL).* Vol. 34. Edited by Alois Goldbacher. Vienna: F. Tempsky, 1895.

Bennett, William Holmes, ed. and trans. *The Gothic Commentary on the Gospel of John: Skeireins aiwaggeljons þairh iohannen: A Decipherment, Edition, and Translation.* New York: Modern Language Association of America, 1960.

Beowulf. *Klaeber's Beowulf and The Fight at Finnsburg.* Edited by Robert Dennis Fulk, Robert E. Bjork, and John D. Niles. 4th ed. Toronto: University of Toronto Press, 2008.

*Brižinski spomeniki: Znanstvenokritična izdaja.* Edited by Jože Faganel et al. Ljubljana, Slovenia: Znanstvenoraziskovalni center SAZU, Inštitut za slovensko literaturo in literarne vede, 1993.

*Capitularia Regum Francorum II*, 1. Edited by Alfred Boretius and Victor Krause. *MGH Legum Sectio II*. Hanover, 1939.

Cassiodorus. *Cassiodori Senatoris Variae*. Edited by Theodor Mommsen. *MGH Auctores antiquissimi*, 12. Berlin: Weidmann, 1894.

———. "De institutione divinarum litterarum, I, 15." In Cassiodorus, *Cassiodori senatoris Institutiones*, edited by Roger Aubrey Baskerville Mynors, 41–51. Oxford: Clarendon Press of Oxford University Press, 1937.

*La Chanson de Roland—The Song of Roland: The French Corpus*. Edited by Joseph J. Duggan. Turnhout, Belgium: Brepols, 2006.

*Concilium Francofurtense*. Edited by Albert Werminghoff. *MGH Concilia*, 2, part 1. Hanover: Hahn, 1906.

*Concilium Turonense anno 813, Concilia Aevi Karolini*. Edited by Albert Werminghoff. *MGH Concilia*, 2, part 1. Hanover: Hahn, 1905.

Condillac, Étienne Bonnot de. "Essai sur l'origine des connaissances humaines." In *Œuvres philosophiques de Condillac*, edited by Georges Le Roy, vol. 1, part II, section I, chapter 15, no. 143, 1–118. Paris: Presses universitaires de France, 1947.

Cook, Albert S., and Chauncey B. Tinker, trans. *Select Translations from Old English Prose*. Boston: Ginn, 1908.

Fichte, Johann Gottlieb. *Reden an die deutsche Nation*. Edited by Alexander Aichele. Hamburg: Felix Meiner Verlag, 2008.

Graff, Eberhard Gottlieb. *Diutiska, Denkmäler deutscher Sprache und Literatur aus alten Handschriften*. 3 vols. Stuttgart: J. G. Cotta'schen Buchhandlung, 1826–29.

Gregory VII. *Das Register Gregors*. Edited by Erich. Caspar. *MGH Epistolae Selectae* 2. Berlin: Weidmann, 1923.

Grimm, Wilhelm. Introduction to *Ruolandes Liet*. Göttingen: Verlag der Dieterichischen Buchhandlung, 1838.

Hafs ibn Albar al Quti. *Le psautier mozarabe de Hafs le Goth*. Edited and translated by Marie Thérèse Urvboy. Toulouse: Presses universitaires du Mirail, 1994.

"Hamelburger Markbeschreibung." In *Althochdeutsches Lesebuch*, edited by Wilhelm Braune and Karl Helm, 6. 16th ed. Revised by Ernst A. Ebbinghaus. Tübingen: Max Niemeyer Verlag, 1979.

*Historia Salonitana Maior*. Edited by Nada Klaić. Belgrade: Naučno delo, 1967.

Iohannes Victoriensis. *Liber Certarum historiarum*. In *MGH Scriptores rerum Germanicarum in usum scholarum separatim editi 36/1*, edited by Fedor Schneider. Hanover: Hahn, 1910.

Irenaeus of Lyon. *Adversus Haerese Irénée de Lyon, Contre les hérésies*. Edited by Adelin Rousseau and Louis Doutreleau. 5 vols. Paris: Cerf, 1965–82.

John VIII. *Regestum Iohannes VIII. Papae*. Edited by Erich Caspar. *MGH Epistolae 7*. Berlin: Weidmann, 1928.

Jerome. *Sancti Eudebii Hieronymi epistulae I, Corpus scriptorum ecclesiasticorum latinorum (CSEL)*. Vol. 54. Edited by Isidor Hilberg. Vienna: F. Tempsky, 1910.

Lo Monaco, Francesco, and Claudia Villa, eds. *I giuramenti di Strasburgo: Testi e tradizione / The Strasbourg Oaths: Texts and Transmission*. Florence: Sismel Edizioni del Galluzzo, 2009.

Massmann, Hans Ferdinand, ed. *Skeireins aiwaggeljons þairh ïohannen, Auslegung des Evangelii Johannis in gothischer Sprache. Aus römischen und mayländischen Handschriften nebst lateinischer Uebersetzung, belegenden Anmerkungen, geschichtlicher Untersuchung, gothisch-lateinischem Wörterbuche und Schriftproben. Im Auftrage Seiner Königlichen Hoheit des Kronprinzen Maximilian von Bayern erlesen, erläutert und zum ersten Male herausgegeben.* Munich: Verlag von George Jaquet, 1834.

Michel, Francisque. *Anglo-Norman Poem on the Conquest of Ireland*. London: William Pickering, 1837.

———. *Bibliothèque Anglo-Saxonne*. Paris: Silvestre, 1837.

———. *Chanson de Roland ou de Roncevaux*. Paris: Silvestre, 1837.

Nithard. *Historiarum Libri III*, 3,5. In *MGH Scriptores rerum Germanicarum in usum scholarum separatim editi 44*, edited by Ernest Müller. Hanover: Hahn, 1907.

Otfrid of Weissenburg. *Otfrids Evangelienbuch*. Edited by Oskar Erdman. 4th ed. revised by Ludwig Wolff. Tübingen: Niemeyer, 1962.

Ottokar. "Ottokars Österreichische Reimchronik," Edited by Joseph Seemüller. *MGH Deutsche Chroniken*, 5, part 1. Hanover, 1890.

"Reginonis abbatis Prumiensis Chronicon cum continuatione Treverensi," *Epistula Reginonis ad Hathonem Archiepiscopum Missa, Prefatio Operis Subsequentis*, xix–xx. In *MGH Scriptores rerum Germanicarum in usum scholarum separatim editi* 50, edited by Friedrich Kurze. Hanover: Hahn, 1890.

Salvian. *De gubernatione Dei, Libri VIII*. Edited by Carolus Halm. *MGH Auctores Antiquissimi* 1, 1. Berlin: Weidmann, 1877.

Sidonius Apollinaris. "Epistulae 4.17." In *Lettres (Livres I–V)*, vol. 2 of *Sidoine Apollinaire*, edited by André Loyen, 149–50. Paris: Belles Lettres, 1970.

———. "Epistulae 5.5." In *Lettres (Livres I–V)*, vol. 2 of *Sidoine Apollinaire*, edited by André Loyen, 180–81. Paris: Belles Lettres, 1970.

Stephanus V. "Epistola ad Zuentopolcum regem." In *Patrologia Latina*, 129, col. 804.

Thomas of Split. *Archdeacon Thomas of Split, History of the Bishops of Salona and Split*. Latin text edited and translated by Olga Pereć, Damir Karbić, Mirjana Matijević Sokol, and James Ross Sweeney. Budapest: Central European Press, 2006.

Tyrwhitt, Thomas. *The Canterbury Tales of Chaucer: To Which Are Added an Essay upon His Language and Versification, an Introductory Discourse, and Notes*. 4 vols. London: T. Payne, 1775–78.

Wace. *Le Roman de Rou*. Edited by A. J. Holden. 3 vols. Paris: Éditions A. and J. Picard, 1970–73.

Walafrid Strabo. *Walahfrid Strabo libellus de exordiis et incrementis quarundam in observationibus ecclesiasticis rerum*. Edited and translated by Alice L. Harting-Correa. Leiden: Brill, 1996.

"Würzburger Markebeschreibung." In *Althochdeutsches Lesebuch*,

edited by Wilhelm Braune and Karl Helm, 6–8. 16th ed. Revised
by Ernst A. Ebbinghaus. Tübingen: Max Niemeyer Verlag, 1979.

SECONDARY SOURCES

Aarsleff, Hans. "The Tradition of Condillac: The Problem of the
    Origin of Language in the Eighteenth Century and the Debate
    in the Berlin Academy before Herder." In Hans Aarsleff, *From
    Locke to Saussure: Essays on the Study of Language and Intellectual
    History*. 146–209. Minneapolis: University of Minnesota Press,
    1982.
Adams, James Noel. *Bilingualism and the Latin Language*.
    Cambridge: Cambridge University Press, 2003.
Althoff, Gerd. *Spielregeln der Politik im Mittelalter: Kommunikation in
    Frieden und Fehde*. Darmstadt: Primus, 1997.
Amory, Patrick. *People and Identity in Ostrogothic Italy, 489–554*.
    Cambridge: Cambridge University Press, 2004.
Auerbach, Erich. *Literary Language and Its Public in Late Latin
    Antiquity and in the Middle Ages*. Translated by Ralph Manheim.
    New York: Pantheon, 1965.
Banniard, Michel. "Acrolecte et identité culturelle en Francia
    carolingienne (VIIIe–IXe s)." In *Sprache und Identität im frühen
    Mittelalter*, edited by Walter Pohl and Bernhard Zeller, 109–20.
    Vienna: Verlag der Österreichen Akademie der Wissenschaften,
    2012.
———. "Théorie et pratique de la langue et du style chez Alcuin:
    Rusticité feinte et rusticité masquée." *Francia* 13 (1986): 579–601.
———. *Viva voce: Communication écrite et communication orale
    du IVe au IXe siècle en Occident latin*. Paris: Institut des études
    augustiniennes, 1992.
——— and Marc Van Uytfanghe. "Consciousness of a Linguistic
    Dichotomy in Carolingian Gaul." In *Latin and the Romance
    Languages in the Early Middle Ages*, edited by Roger Wright,
    114–29. London: Routledge, 1991.

Bäuml, Franz. "Medieval Texts and the Two Theories of Oral-Formulaic Composition: A Proposal for a Third Theory." *New Literary History* 16 (1984–85): 31–49.

Bekker-Nielsen, Hans, and Ole Widding. *Arne Magnusson, the Manuscript Collector*, translated by Robert W. Mattila. Odense, Denmark: Odense University Press, 1972.

Belmon, Jérôme, and Françoise Veillard. "Latin farci et occitan dans les actes du XIe siècle." *Pratiques de l'écrit documentaire au XIe siècle* 155 (1997): 149–83.

Bloch, R. Howard. "The First Document and the Birth of Medieval Studies." In *A New History of French Literature*, edited by Denis Hollier, 6–13. Cambridge: Harvard University Press, 1989.

———. *A Needle in the Right Hand of God: The Norman Conquest of 1066 and the Making and Meaning of the Bayeux Tapestry*. New York: Random House, 2006.

Booker, Courtney M. "History, Identity, and the First French Text: Nithard's *Historiae* and the Politics of Value." Paper presented at the annual meeting of the American Historical Association, New York, 4 January 2009.

Brakelmann, Julius. "Die Nithardhandschrift und die Eide von Strassburg." *Zeitschrift für deutsche Philologie* 3 (1871): 85–94.

Brown, Dennis. *Vir Trilinguis: A Study in the Biblical Exegesis of Saint Jerome*. Kampen, the Netherlands: Kok Pharos, 1992.

Brown, Peter. *Power and Persuasion in Late Antiquity: Towards a Christian Empire*. Madison: University of Wisconsin Press, 1992.

Brunner, Thomas. "Le passage aux langues vernaculaires dans les actes de la pratique en Occident." *Le Moyen Âge* 115 (2009): 29–72.

Carrannante, Antonio. "Mai, Angelo." In *Dizionario biografico degli Italiani*, 67:517–20. Rome: Istituto della Enciclopedia italiana, 2006.

Christys, Ann. "How Can I Trust You, Since You Are a Christian and I Am a Moor?" In *Texts and Identities in the Early Middle Ages*, edited by Richard Corradini, Rob Meens, Christina Pössel, and Philip Shaw, 359–72. Vienna: Verlag der Österreichischer Akademie der Wissenschaften, 2006.

Cowdery, Herbert Edward John. "Pope Gregory VII (1073–85) and the Liturgy." *Journal of Theological Studies*, n.s., 55, no. 1 (2004): 55–83.

Davis, Kathleen. "The Performance of Translation Theory in King Alfred's National Literary Program." In *Manuscript, Narrative, Lexicon: Essays on Literary and Cultural Transmission in Honor of Whitney F. Bolton*, edited by Robert Boenig and Kathleen Davis, 149–70. Lewisburg, PA: Bucknell University Press, 2000.

De Jong, Mayke. "Some Reflections on Mandarin Language." In *East and West: Modes of Communication*, edited by Euangelos Chrysos and Ian Wood, 61–69. Leiden: Brill, 1999.

De la Rue, Gervais. *Essais historiques sur les bardes, les jongleurs et les trouvères normands et anglo-normands, suivis de pièces de Malherbe, qu'on ne trouve dans aucune édition de ses oeuvres*. Vol. 2. Caen, France: Mancel, 1834.

Discenza, Nicole Guenther. "Alfred's Verse Preface to the Pastoral Care and the Chain of Authority." *Neophilologus* 84, no. 4 (2001): 625–33.

Dobrovský, Josef. "Nachricht von drey slawischen Aufsätzen, welche in einer sehr alten lateinischen Handschrift der öffentlichen Bibliothek zu München gefunden worden sind." In Josef Dobrovský, *Slovanka: Zur Kenntniss der alten und neuen slawischen Literatur, der Sprachkunde nach allen Mundarten, der Geschichte und Alterthümer*, 249–51. Prague: In der herrlschen Buchhandlung, 1814.

Docen, Bernhard Joseph. "Nachrichten von einigen alten Handschriften der ehemaligen Freysinger Stiftsbibliothek." In *Beyträge zur Geschichte und Literatur, vorzüglich aus den Schätzen der pfalzbaierischen Centralbibliothek zu München*, edited by Johann Christoph Freiherr von Aretin, 7:225–59, 509–34. Munich: In Kommission der Sehererschen Kunst-und Buchhandlung, 1806.

Dolezal, Helmut, "Endlicher, Stephan Ladislaus." In *Neue Deutsche Biographie* (1959). http://www.deutsche-biographie.de/pnd100122434.html.

Dolinar, Darko. "Slovene Text Editions, Slavic Philology and Nation-Building." In *Editing the Nation's Memory: Textual Scholarship and Nation-Building in 19th-Century Europe*, edited by Dirk Van Hulle and Joep Leerssen, 65–78. Amsterdam: Rodopi, 2008.

Dröll, Regina Maria. "Sprachwahl als Indikator politischer Standortbestimmung im 'deutschen' Mittelalter: Der Umgang mit der Volkssprache von den Karolingern zu den Staufern." PhD diss., Johann Wolfgang Goethe Universität, 2005.

Endlicher, Stephan, and August Heinrich Hoffmann von Fallersleben. *Fragmenta Theotisca versionis antiquissimae evangelii S. Matthaei et aliquot homiliarum. E Membranis Monseensibus Bibliothecae Palatinae Vindobonensis.* Vienna: Typis Caroli Gerold, 1834.

Fine, John A. V., Jr. *The Early Medieval Balkans: A Critical Survey from the Sixth to the Late Twelfth Century.* Ann Arbor: University of Michigan Press, 1991.

Fjalldal, Magnús. "To Fall by Ambition: Grímur Thorkelín and His Beowulf Edition." *Neophilologus* 92, no. 2 (2008): 321–32.

Frank, Roberta. "A Scandal in Toronto: The Dating of Beowulf a Quarter Century On." *Speculum* 82, no. 4 (2007): 843–64.

Geary, Patrick J. "Land, Language and Memory in Europe 700–1100." *Transactions of the Royal Historical Society*, 6th series, 9 (1999): 169–84.

———. "Oathtaking and Conflict Management in the Ninth Century." In *Rechtsverständnis und Handlungsstrategien im mittelalterlichen Konfliktaustrag: Festschrift für Hanna Vollrath*, edited by Stefan Esders and Christine Reinle, 239–53. Munich: Böhlau, 2007.

Godden, Malcolm. "The Alfredian Project and Its Aftermath:

Rethinking the Literary History of the Ninth and Tenth
Centuries." *Proceedings of the British Academy* 162 (2009): 93–122.

Goyens, Michèle, and Werner Verbeke, eds. *The Dawn of the
Written Vernacular in Western Europe*. Leuven, Belgium: Leuven
University Press, 2003.

Graff, Eberhard Gottlieb. *Althochdeutscher Sprachschatz oder,
Wörterbuch der althochdeutschen Sprache*. 6 vols. Berlin: beim
Verfasser und in Commission der Nikolaischen Buchhandlung,
1834–42.

———. *Diutiska: Denkmäler deutscher Sprache und Literatur aus alten
Handschriften*. 3 vols. Stuttgart: J. G. Cotta'schen Buchhandlung,
1826–29.

Gribomont, Jean, and Jean Mallet. "Le latin biblique aux mains des
barbares: Les manuscrits UEST des Prophètes." *Romanobarbarica*
4 (1979): 35–105.

Hahn, Josef. *Bartholomäus Kopitar und seine Beziehungen zu
München*. Munich: R. Trofenik, 1982.

Halsall, Guy. *Barbarian Migrations and the Roman West 367–568*.
Cambridge: Cambridge University Press, 2008.

Haubrichs, Wolfgang. "Differenz und Identität—Sprache als
Instrument der Kommunikation und der Gruppenbildung im
frühen Mittelalter." In *Sprache und Identität im frühen Mittelalter*,
edited by Walter Pohl and Bernhard Zeller, 23–38. Vienna: Verlag
der Österreichen Akademie der Wissenschaften, 2012.

———. "Ethnizität zwischen Differenz und Identität. Sprache
als Instrument der Kommunikation und der Gruppenbildung
im frühen Mittelalter." *Zeitschrift für Literaturwissenschaft und
Linguistik* 164 (2011): 10–38.

Heim, Rudolf-Dieter. *Romanen und Germanen in Charlemagnes
Reich: Untersuchungen zur Benennung romanischer und
germanischer Völker, Sprache und Länder in französischen
Dichtungen des Mittelalters*. Munich: Fink, 1984.

Henss, Walter. "Die Integrität der Bibelübersetzung im religiösen

Denken des 5. Jahrhunderts." In *The Bible and Medieval Culture*, edited by Willem Lourdaux and Daniël Verhelst, 25–57. Leuven, Belgium: Leuven University Press, 1979.

Hirschi, Caspar. *Wettkampf der Nationen: Konstruktionen einer deutschen Ehrgemeinschaft an der Wende vom Mittelalter zur Neuzeit*. Göttingen: Wallstein, 2005.

Hobson, Anthony. "Appropriations from Foreign Libraries during the French Revolution and Empire." *Bulletin du bibliophile*, no. 2 (1989): 255–72.

Hummer, Hans J. *Politics and Power in Early Medieval Europe*. Cambridge: Cambridge University Press, 2005.

Hurt, James. *Ælfric*. New York: Twayne, 1972.

Joseph, John E. "842, 1871 and All That: Alsace-Lorraine and the Transformations of Linguistic Nationalism." In *The French Language and Questions of Identity*, edited by Wendy Ayres-Bennett and Mari C. Jones, 44–52. London: Legenda, 2007.

Karg-Gasterstädt, Elizabeth. "Graff, Eberhard Gottlieb." In *Neue Deutsche Biographie* 6:730. http://www.deutsche-biographie.de.

Keppen, Petr, ed. *Sobranie slovenskih pamjatnikov, nahodjaščihsja vně Rossii*. Book 1, *Pamjatniki sobrannye v Germanii*. St. Petersburg: Tipografia Imperatorskago vospitatel'nago doma, 1827.

Kopitar, Bartholomäus. *B. Kopitars Briefwechsel mit Jakob Grimm*. Edited by Max Vasmer. Vienna: Böhlau, 1987.

———. *Glagolita Clozianus*. Vienna: Carolus Gerold Bibliopola, 1836.

———. *Grammatik der slavischen Sprache in Krain, Kärnten und Steyermark*. Laibach (Ljubljana), Slovenia: W. H. Korn, 1808.

Kos, Janko, et al., eds. *Zbornik Brižinski spomeniki*. Ljubljana, Slovenia: Znanstvenoraziskovalni center SAZU, Inštitut za slovensko literaturo in literarne vede, 1996.

Krotz, Elke. "Hear saget fona gotspelle Zur äußeren und inneren Kohärenz einer lateinisch-althochdeutschen Sammelhandschrift." In *Volkssprachig-lateinische Mischtexte und Textensembles in der althochdeutschen, altsächsischen und altenglischen Überlieferung: Mediävistisches Kolloquium des*

*Zentrums für Mittelalterstudien der Otto-Friedrich-Universität
Bamberg am 16. und 17. November 2001*, edited by Rolf Bergmann,
175–86. Heidelberg: Universitätsverlag, 2003.

Laffitte, Marie Pierre. "La Bibliothèque nationale et les 'conquêtes
artistiques' de la Révolution et de l'Empire: les manuscrits
d'Italie (1796–1815)." *Bulletin du bibliophile*, no. 2 (1989): 273–323.

Leerssen, Joep. "Introduction: Philology and the European
Construction of National Literatures." In *Editing the Nation's
Memory: Textual Scholarship and Nation-Building in 19th-Century
Europe*, edited by Dirk Van Hulle and Joep Leerssen, 13–27.
Amsterdam: Rodopi, 2008.

———. "Literary Historicism: Romanticism, Philologists, and the
Presence of the Past." *Modern Language Quarterly* 65, no. 2 (2004):
221–43.

Legrand, Robert. *Guizot et son temps: propos et portraits*. Abbeville,
France: F. Paillart, 2002.

Lhotsky, Alphons. "Zur Frühgeschichte der Wiener
Hofbibliothek." In Alphons Lhotsky, *Europäisches Mittelalter:
Das Land Österreich*, vol. 1 of *Aufsätze und Vorträge*, edited by
Hans Wagner and Heinrich Koller, 149–93. Munich: Oldenbourg,
1970.

Lowe, Kathryn A. "The Development of the Anglo-Saxon
Boundary Clause." *Nomina* 21 (1998): 63–100.

Lusignan, Serge. *La langue des rois au Moyen Age: Le français en France
et en Angleterre*. Paris: Presses universitaires de France, 2004.

Machan, Tim William. *English in the Middle Ages*. Oxford: Oxford
University Press, 2003.

Massmann, Hans Ferdinand. *Kurze und wahrhaftige Beschreibung des
grossen Burschenfestes auf der Wartburg bei Eisenach am 18ten und
19ten Siegesmonds 1817*. Jena: Frommann, 1817.

McKitterick, Rosamond. "Latin and Romance: An Historian's
Perspective." In *Latin and the Romance Languages in the Early
Middle Ages*, edited by Roger Wright, 130–45. London: Routledge,
1991.

———, ed. *The New Cambridge Medieval History*. Vol. 2, *c.700–c. 900*. Cambridge: Cambridge University Press, 1995.

Merchiers, Ingrid. *Cultural Nationalism in the South Slav Habsburg Lands in the Early Nineteenth Century: The Scholarly Network of Jernej Kopitar (1780–1844)*. Munich: Verlag Otto Sagner, 2007.

Müller, Hans-Harald. "Die Lebendigen und die Untoten: Lassen sich Auseinandersetzungen zwischen Wissenschaftskonzeptionen als 'Kontroversen' rekonstruieren? Am Beispiel von Positivismus und Geistesgeschichte." In *Kontroversen in der Literaturtheorie/Literaturtheorie in der Kontroverse*, edited by Ralf Klausnitzer and Carlos Spoerhase, 171–82. Bern: Lang, 2007.

Müller, Stephan. *Vom Annolied zur Kaiserchronik: Zu Text-und Forschungsgeschichte einer verlorenen deutschen Reimchronik*. Heidelberg: Universitätsverlag C. Winter, 1999.

Muntz, Eugène. "Les invasions de 1814–1815 et la spoliation de nos musées (Épisodes d'histoire diplomatique)." *La Nouvelle Revue*, April 1897, 703–16; July 1897, 193–207; August 1897, 420–39.

Nelson, Janet L. "Public Histories and Private History in the Work of Nithard." *Speculum* 60, no. 2 (1985): 251–93.

O'Donnell, James Joseph. *Augustine: A New Biography*. New York: HarperCollins, 2005.

———. *Cassiodorus*. Berkeley: University of California Press, 1979. Post print 1995, http://www9.georgetown.edu/faculty/jod/ texts/cassbook/toc.html.

Pankow, Christiane. *Die Wirkung der Deutschen Grammatik von Jacob Grimm auf die grammatischen Ansichten russischer Sprachforscher im 19. Jahrhundert*. Tübingen: G. Narr, 2002.

Rabuck, Mark. "The Imagined Boundary: Borders and Frontiers in Anglo-Saxon England." PhD diss., Yale University, 1996.

"La résistible ascension des vulgaires. Contacts entre latin et langues vulgaires au bas Moyen Âge. Problèmes pour l'historien." *Mélanges de l'École française de Rome—Moyen Âge* 117, no. 2 (2005).

Richter, Joachim Burkhard. *Hans Ferdinand Maßmann: Altdeutscher Patriotismus im 19. Jahrhundert*. Berlin: Walter de Gruyter, 1992.

Richter, Michael. "Concept and Evolution of the *Tres linguae sacrae*." In *Language of Religion, Language of the People: Medieval Judaism, Christianity, and Islam*, edited by Ernst Bremer, Jörg Jarnut, Michael Richter, and David Wasserstein. Munich: Wilhelm Fink Verlag, 2006.

Roach, William. "Francisque Michel: A Pioneer in Medieval Studies." *Proceedings of the American Philosophical Society* 114, no. 3 (1970): 168–78.

Sandys, John Edwin. *A History of Classical Scholarship*. Vol. 3. Cambridge: Cambridge University Press, 1908.

Schaefer, Ursula. *Vokalität: Altenglische Dichtung zwischen Mündlichkeit und Schriftlichkeit*. Tübingen: Narr, 1992.

Schäferdiek, Knut. "Die Fragmente der 'Skeireins' und der Johanneskommentar des Theodor von Herakleia." In Knut Schäferdiek, *Schwellenzeit: Beiträge zur Geschichte des Christentums in Spätantike und Frühmittelalter*. 69–88. Berlin: Walter de Gruyter, 1996.

Scherer, Wilhelm. "Graff, Eberhard Gottlieb." In *Allgemeine Deutsche Biographie* 9:566–68 (1879). http://www.deutsche-bio graphie.de/pnd118541374.html?anchor=adb.

Schmidt-Wiegand Ruth. "Hammelburger Markbeschreibungen." In *Die deutsche Literatur des Mittelalters: Verfasserlexikon*, edited by Kurt Ruh et al., 3:427–28. Berlin: Walter de Gruyter, 1981.

———. "Würzburger Markbeschreibungen." In *Die deutsche Literatur des Mittelalters: Verfasserlexikon*, edited by Kurt Ruh et al., 10:1455–58. Berlin: Walter de Gruyter, 1999.

Shippey, Tom. "The Case of Beowulf." In *Editing the Nation's Memory: Textual Scholarship and Nation-Building in 19th-Century Europe*, edited by Dirk Van Hulle and Joep Leerssen, 223–39. Amsterdam: Rodopi, 2008.

———and Andreas Haarder, eds. *Beowulf: The Critical Heritage*. London: Routledge, 1988.

Smith, Julia M. H. *Europe after Rome: A New Cultural History 500–1000*. Oxford: Oxford University Press, 2005.

Sokol, Mirjana Matijević. "Archdeacon Thomas of Split (1200–1268): A Source of Early Croatian History." *Review of Croatian History* 3, no. 1 (2007): 251–70.

Steinmann, Ernst. "Die Plünderung Roms durch Bonaparte." *Internationale Monatsschrift für Wissenschaft, Kunst und Technik* 11, no. 6 (1917): cols. 641–76, 819–75.

Štih, Peter. "Slowenisch, Alpenslawisch oder Slawisch: zwischen Donau und Adria im Frühmittelalter." In *Sprache und Identität im frühen Mittelalter*, edited by Walter Pohl and Bernhard Zeller, 171–83. Vienna: Verlag der Österreichen Akademie der Wissenschaften, 2012.

Taylor, Andrew. "Was There a Song of Roland?," *Speculum* 76, no. 1 (2001): 28–65.

Thomas, Linda, and Shân Wareing, eds. *Language, Society and Power: An Introduction*. London: Routledge, 1999.

Trilling, Renée R. *The Aesthetics of Nostalgia: Historical Representation in Old English Verse*. Toronto: University of Toronto Press, 2009.

Trotter, David. "'Si le français n'y peut aller': Villers-Cotterêts and Mixed-Language Documents from the Pyrenees." In *Conceptions of Europe in Renaissance France*, edited by David Cowling, 77–97. Amsterdam: Rodopi, 2006.

Urla, Jacqueline. "Ethnic Protest and Social Planning: A Look at Basque Language Revival." *Cultural Anthropology* 3, no. 4 (1988): 379–94.

Valensise, Marina, ed. *François Guizot et la culture politique de son temps: colloque de la Fondation Guizot-Val Richer*. Paris: Gallimard and Le Seuil, 1991.

Van Acker, Marieke, Rika van Deyck, and Marc van Uytfanghe, eds. *Latin écrit—roman oral? De la dichotomisation à la continuité*. *Corpus Christianorum, Lingua Patrum*, 5. Turnhout, Belgium: Brepols, 2008.

Vollrath, Hannah. "Rechtstexte in der oralen Rechtskultur des frühen Mittelalters." In *Mittelalterforschung nach der Wende 1989*, edited by Michael Borgolte, 319–48. Munich: R. Oldenbourg Verlag, 1995.

Vostokov, Alexandr Khristoforovich. "Rassuždenie o slavjanskom jazyke." *Trud obshhestva ljubitelej rossijskoj slovesnosti pri Imperatorskom Moskovskom universitete* 17 (1820): 9–10, 15–27.

Wolfram, Herwig. *Gotische Studien: Volk und Herrschaft im frühen Mittelalter*. Munich: Beck, 2005.

———. "Meinungsbildung und Propaganda im österreichischen Mittelalter." In *Öffentliche Meinung in der Geschichte Österreichs*, edited by Erich Zöllner, 14–26. Vienna: Österreichische Bundesverlag, 1979.

Wright, Roger. *Late Latin and Early Romance in Spain and Carolingian France*. Liverpool: Cairns, 1982.

———, ed. *Latin and the Romance Languages in the Early Middle Ages*. London: Routledge, 1991.

———. "Linguistic and Ethnic Identities in the Iberian Peninsula (400–1000 A.D.)." In *Sprache und Identität im frühen Mittelalter*, edited by Walter Pohl and Bernhard Zeller, 99–108. Vienna: Verlag der Österreichen Akademie der Wissenschaften, 2012.

———. "La période de transition du latin, de la lingua Romana et du français." *Médiévales* 45 (2003): 11–23.

———. "Translation between Latin and Romance in the Early Middle Ages." In *Translation Theory and Practice in the Middle Ages*, edited by Jeanette Beer, 7–32. Kalamazoo: Medieval Institute Publications, Western Michigan University, 1997.

# Index

Mourcin, Joseph-Jean-Théophile de, 69
Mozarabic liturgy, 54
Müller, Hans-Harald, 79n11
Müller, Karl, 25
Müller, Stephan, 17
Munich royal library, 22

Napoleon (Bonaparte), 21, 25
Napoleonic Code, 27
Napoleonic wars, 7, 15, 25, 69
national identity: German, 4
nationalism, 14, 59, 72–73; Danish, and Thorkelín's *Beowulf,* 31–32; German, 24, 26; and language, 12–14
national traditions, construction of, 15, 35–37
Nelson, Janet, 70
*Nibelungenlied,* 27–28
nineteenth century, and construction of "Middle Ages," 12–37
Nithard, 69–70
Nodier, Charles, 29–30

oaths, 66–72; of Koblenz, 68, 71–72; of Strasbourg, 68–71
Old Church Slavonic language, 21–23, 32
Old English Heptateuch, 49
Old French language, 30
Old High German language, 24–25, 45–46, 65–68
Old Norse language, 19–20, 31
Old Slovenian language, 32

Osten-Sacken, Baron von, 23
Otfrid of Weissenburg, 47, 54, 72
*Otfrids Evangelienbuch,* 47, 72
Ottokar II, King of Bohemia, 58
Outzen, Nicholaus, 32
Oxford, 31
Oxford University, 33; Bodleian Library MS Digby 23, 31

paleography, Mai and, 17–19
palimpsests, 18–19, 28–29
paraphrase, of scripture, 50
Paris, 21, 25, 29–30
patristic literature, Greek, 36
patronage, 20, 22
*Patrum nova collectio,* 19
Paul, Saint, 46
Pertz, Georg Heinrich, 82n37
philologists: and construction of "Middle Ages," 12–37; German, 59, 66
philology: German Romantic, 6; Indo-European, 14, 36; new, of nineteenth century, 17
Priscillianism, 54
Prussia, 27
psalter, 47–48
publishers, 30
Punic language, 39–40, 60

record keeping, and use of vernacular languages, 56–73
rediscovery of ancient / medieval texts, 11–12, 20–21, 24, 27, 29–31, 77n4; Cicero's *De re publica,* 18; Freising Fragments, 22–23;

Patrick J. Geary, *Language and Power in the Early Middle Ages*

G. W. Bowersock, *Empires in Collision in Late Antiquity*

Sanjay Subrahmanyam, *Three Ways to Be Alien:
Travails and Encounters in the Early Modern World*

Jürgen Kocka, *Civil Society and Dictatorship
in Modern German History*

Heinz Schilling, *Early Modern European Civilization
and Its Political and Cultural Dynamism*

Brian Stock, *Ethics through Literature:
Ascetic and Aesthetic Reading in Western Culture*

Fergus Millar, *The Roman Republic in Political Thought*

Peter Brown, *Poverty and Leadership in the Later Roman Empire*

Anthony D. Smith, *The Nation in History:
Historiographical Debates about Ethnicity and Nationalism*

Carlo Ginzburg, *History, Rhetoric, and Proof*